Terrorists
or
Freedom
Fighters

Edited by **Ely Tavin
and Yonah Alexander**

**Published in cooperation with
Department of Education and Culture,
World Zionist Organization
and
Institute for Studies on International
Terrorism, State University of New York**

**HERO Books
Fairfax, Virginia**

For information, address:

**HERO BOOKS
Suite 400
8316 Arlington Blvd
Fairfax, VA 22031
703-560-6427**

Manufactured in the United States of America

ISBN 0-915979-19-5

CONTENTS

PREFACE   vii
    Dr. Eli Tavin, Head, Department of Education and
    Culture, World Zionist Organization, Jerusalem, Israel

INTRODUCTION   xi
    Professor Y. Alexander, Director, Institute for Studies
    in International Terrorism, State University of New
    York

Part One   An Overview

OVERVIEWS   3
    Professor B. Akzin, Hebrew University, Jerusalem, Israel
    General (Res) A. Yariv, Director of Center for Strategic
    Studies, Tel Aviv University, Tel Aviv, Israel

CHAPTER I   **The Ethical Issue**   5
    Professor E. Rackman, President Bar Ilan University,
    Ramat Gan, Israel

CHAPTER II   **Terrorists or Freedom Fighters**   12
    Professor M. Arens, Former Minister of Defense, Israel

Part Two   International Perspective

CHAPTER III **State Sponsored Terrorism**   21
    R. Cline, Center for Strategic and International Studies,
    Georgetown University, Washington, D.C.
    Y. Alexander, Institute for Studies in International
    Terrorism, State University of New York

CHAPTER IV **International Terrorism and UN   40
            Responses**
    Dr. A. Gerson, Special Assistant to the U.S. Ambassador
    to the U.N., New York, N.Y.

Part III   Jewish Perspective

CHAPTER V   **The Hagana and the War for**   **51**
               Israel's Independence
Dr. N. Lorch, Harry S. Truman Institute for the Advance-
ment of Peace, Hebrew University, Jerusalem, Israel

CHAPTER VI   **The IZL and Its Role in the**   **58**
               Liberation of Israel from the
               British Rule
Professor J. Nedava, Haifa University, Haifa, Israel

CHAPTER VII   **Lechi's Share in the Struggle**   **66**
               for Israel's Liberation
Dr. Z. Iviansky, Kibbutz Eyn-Charod (Meuchad)

Part IV   Third World Perspective

CHAPTER VIII **The Middle East Experience**   **83**
Professor M. Maoz, Hebrew University, Jerusalem, Israel

CHAPTER IX   **Terrorists and Guerrillas in Africa**   **90**
J. Lisker, Subcommittee on Security and Terrorism, U.S.
Senate, Washington, D.C.

Part V   Western Experience

CHAPTER X   **European Terrorism**   **113**
Professor J. Sundberg, School of International Law,
University of Stockholm, Stockholm, Sweden

CHAPTER XI   **French Democracy versus**   **124**
               Terrorism: Attitudes, Policy,
               Laws, and the Press
Professor C. Franck, Department of Constitutional Law
and Political Science, University of Paris 1, Paris,
France

Part VI Future Perspectives

CHAPTER XII **Unconventional Terrorism--A**   **133**
                 Glance into the Future
   Professor Y. Dror, Hebrew University, Jerusalem, Israel

CHAPTER XIII **Summary: From Global War to**   **141**
                 Terrorism
   Professor Y. Ne'eman, Former Minister of Science and
   Development, Israel

CONCLUSION **Terrorists and Freedom Fighters**   **145**

BIBLIOGRAPHY   **147**

PREFACE

This work is most appropriate since 1984 marks the 40th anniversary of the Jewish revolt against the British rule in Palestine. "Tenuat Hameri," the resistance movement (the Haganah, Etzel, and Lehi), in its struggle for an independent Jewish state, realized that the establishment of a distinct national home in Palestine was not only an acute necessity but also a prerequisite for the very survival of the entire Jewish nation. Clearly, this revolt against foreign rule was a classic case of a national liberation movement striving to save a people from extermination.

Today there are those who are still trying to equate the Jewish freedom fighters of that historical period with present-day terrorists. Nothing can be further from the truth.

Contemporary terrorists constitute a radical break with reality. They operate outside the basic rules of civilization, while holding contempt for the legal and moral norms of all societies. These outlaws glorify violent deeds for the sake of their own sanctified cause. The Palestine Liberation Organization (PLO) characterizes the nature of this grave trend of our time. One has only to look at the Palestinian National Charter which calls for the elimination of Israel. This goal, coupled with the PLO violence in the Middle East and elsewhere testifies to the true PLO nature.

Nevertheless, the question of who are the terrorists is still being debated. The definitions of ideological and political violence have evaded a clear understanding of this important problem. Terms such as "people's war," "crusaders," "commanders," and "guerrillas" are used interchangeably because of semantic confusion, which obscures the true meaning of the terrorist threat to our civilization. A reason contributing to the lack of a universally accepted definition of terrorism is the moral crisis of the world community. Ideological and political violence is an organized attack against innocent civilians. Such activity should produce widespread revulsion, yet states tolerate, appease, and glorify terrorists as heroes, and sponsor various terrorist movements all over the world. There seems to be a widespread erosion of a moral link between means and ends, however just the real or proclaimed cause of a terrorist group might be.   As long as a morally confused society neglects the human rights of the noncombatant population, the borderline between plain terrorism and justified violence will continue to remain blurred.

Thus far, thousands of innocent people have been victimized, killed, and maimed as a result of terrorism. According to available data, from 1970 to 1984 over 20,000 domestic and international terrorist incidents occurred.   A total of some 30,000 individuals have been killed and over 20,000 wounded, with property damage in billions of dollars. These casualties have included government officials, politicians, judges, diplomats, business executives, labor leaders, university professors, college students, school children, travelers, pilgrims, and olympic athletes.

The advances of science and technology are slowly turning everyone in our modern society into a potential victim of terrorism, with no immunity for the noncombatants of the world or for those nations and peoples who have no direct connection to particular conflicts, or to specific grievances that motivate acts of violence.   What is of particular concern is the fact that terrorism is escalating into the struggle-for-power process as a form of surrogate warfare, whereby small groups with direct and indirect state support are able to conduct political warfare at the national level, and ultimately may even succeed in altering the balance-of-power on the international level.   Some keen observers of this new phenomenon have noted:

In the face of this danger, people in democratic societies need to understand the nature of contemporary terrorism in order to find constructive approaches to deal with it.   The major concerns to be dealt with are:

- What is the nature of the terrorist threat?
- Is there a terrorist personality?
- Can there be a cultural offensive against terrorism?

- What ideas can we produce for the younger generations to immunize them against the temptations of terrorism?
- How can the information media be of use in combating terrorism?

Undoubtedly, deliberations will advance our intellectual insights, increase our awareness, and recommend ways and means on national, regional, and global levels to cope with this destructive wave which threatens the very survival of humanity.

Eli Tavin
Tel Aviv, Israel

INTRODUCTION

Unlike their historical counterparts, present-day terrorists have introduced into contemporary life a new breed
of violence in terms of technology, victimization, threat,
and response. The globalization and brutalization of
modern violence make it abundantly clear that we have
entered a new "Age of Terrorism" with all its frightening
ramifications.

The statistics are, indeed, staggering. The number of
terrorist incidents involving fatalities has been increasing
about 20 percent a year since the early 1970s. In 1983--
the bloodiest year yet--the figure rose to more than 2,000
casualties.

The distinction between a state of war and a state of
peace is becoming increasingly blurred. Hence, George
Orwell's famous dictum that "peace is war" assumes a
greater sense of reality. Although predictions are hazardous, it is safe to assume that contemporary terrorism as an
expedient tactical and strategic tool of politics in the
struggle for power within and among nations is now an
established mode of conflict. It provides a model for those
with a variety of causes.

The major reason for the continuation and probable
intensification of terrorism is the fact that many of the
roots of ideological and political violence will remain
unresolved and new causes will arise in the coming months
and years. Since technological developments offer new
targets and new capabilities for modern terrorists, future
incidents could be much more costly in terms of human lives
and property.

Modern terrorism poses many threats to contemporary
society and is likely to have a serious impact on the quality
of life and on orderly civilized existence. Perhaps the most
significant dangers are those relating to the safety,
welfare, and rights of ordinary people; the stability of the
state system; the health and pace of economic development;
and the expansion or even the survival of democracy. If
we try to ignore the dangers of contemporary terrorism, as
we are surely tempted to do, the fear and tragedy it causes

can only continue to haunt us.   If we carefully examine its causes and consequences, there is hope that we will find the clues to measures that will enable us to contain, if not eliminate, the devastation of terrorism as a new mode of warfare.

And yet, what constitutes terrorism is highly controversial.   We are reminded of how Gibbon came to grips with the problem of writing about Corsica.   He said that Corsica is easier to deplore than to describe.   Some feel the validity of their cause, such as resistance to colonial or totalitarian regimes justifies the resort to political violence.   They view terrorism as an acceptable alternative to the exercise of legitimate power.   To others, the use of this type of force, regardless of motivation, is a negative and even criminal act--outside the realm of what is tolerable--which therefore necessarily must be punished in accordance with the relevant domestic and international laws.

Yonah Alexander
Washington, DC

PART ONE
AN OVERVIEW

OVERVIEWS
Professor B. Akzin

Of the two terms which play a central role in this work, that of *Freedom Fighters* is the more difficult to define. Many militant advocates of change assume this name, some with good reason, others without. The criteria are subjective rather than objective. What is important to consider is whether genuine freedom fighting entitles its adherents to resort to terror, and it is my belief that the answer to this should be in the negative.

As for *terror*, the term has undergone many changes of meaning. It always meant an unreasonable and cruel exercise of violence, unfortunately a frequent feature in the history of mankind. Governments and their opponents have resorted to it. It is encountered both in relations within given countries and in the context of international relations, especially in times of war. In modern language, the term terror became prominent in the days of the French Revolution, when applied to what is widely regarded as an unreasonable and cruel exercise of violence by French governmental authorities. Terror by governments is still with us, but there we encounter a significant phenomenon: for centuries public opinion has forced governments to limit both the extent and the intensity of its exercise of violence, and there is a growing feeling in open and democratic societies that any such exercise beyond very narrow limits lacks moral legitimacy. Against this, even massive and unrestrained violence--terror, in other words--is often regarded as morally justified if fielded by opponents of established governmental authority, and freedom fighting is often the banner used in order to give it justification. The contradiction between these two opposite trends has been investigated in an article published several years ago.* I believe in the conviction that neither the desire to change an oppressive political regime, nor the redressing social injustice, nor aim of national liberation and freedom

---

* See B. Akzin. Gegenszliche Tendenzen in der Gewaltausubung. In Pawlowski et al., Festschrift fur Konrad Duden, Beck'scher Verlag, Munchen 1977, pp 1-14.

fighting justifies resort to excessive violence which goes
today by the name of terror.

What is this terror? In the 19th and early 20th
centuries the term, when used in the context of anti-
government activities, was applied mainly to violence
directed against active members and heads of the regime
objected to. In other words, individual and selective
terror. Innocent bystanders might suffer from it, but they
were not its intended victims. The moral legitimacy of
even this kind of terror was, and still is, a matter of
controversy. But in recent decades another form of terror,
an indiscriminate, non-selective terror directed mainly
against the general population, has grown and it is often
glorified. This kind of terror as an unmitigated evil must
be eradicated.

General (Res) A. Yariv

Terrorism has become a permanent phenomenon in many
parts of the world, with terrorists often practicing the
indiscriminate use of violence for political purposes. For
the Jewish people in general and for Israelis in particular,
there is a special interest in pointing out the differences
between an underground movement fighting for national
freedom and a terrorist organization. But at the same
time, one should not forget that both fight for a political
purpose.

Israelis have been engaged for the last twenty years in
a continuous struggle with Palestinian terrorism. So far we
have been able to keep it within tolerable limits at a
tolerable price. Considering the relevant circumstances,
this has been no mean achievement. It seems to me that it
should be feasible to maintain this situation as long as we
remember that there is no shortcut to the solution of the
Palestinian problem, and therefore to Palestinian terrorism.
The latter cannot be done away with in one fell swoop.
Only the eventual, political resolution of the Palestinian
problem can put an end to Palestinian terrorism. The
better this is understood, the more effective our combat
against it will be.

CHAPTER I

The
Ethical
Issue

Professor E. Rackman

"Terrorists or Freedom Fighters." Which term describes the brave Jews who 40 years ago created the
underground that forced Britain out of Palestine? Is
today's PLO to be accorded the same status? And what of
all the rebels in Africa, Central America, Ireland,
Afghanistan, and many other places where civil strife
exists?

From Jewish sources one can derive considerable
support for two theses: first, Jewish law recognized that
under certain circumstances one has a right to rebel--to
defy the order of constituted authority whether that
authority is a monarch or a majority--and that right is
protected and enforced by the judiciary of the Jewish
people; and second, within certain limits one can also resort
to violence, but with regard to violence the constraints are
very clear and exacting. The Bible provides for the
appointment of a king, but the king is not to be an absolute
monarch. He is subject to the Law--the Torah. He is not
the legislator; only God is and those who are the custodians
of the Law. Cursing God was a capital offense but cursing
the king was not. Indeed, the Torah provides no
punishment for disobedience to the ruler. One is punished

only for disobedience to God.   The ruler too must function
within the parameters of the Torah as everyone else must,
and the ruler himself can be punished for his breach of the
Law.
     One might call this a constitutional limitation of the
executive authority.   However, when Joshua succeeded
Moses as the Jewish leader, the Jewish people--not God--
extended Joshua's powers.   They promised obedience to his
commands and authorized him to give the death penalty to
anyone who would disobey him.   It is only because of this
that revolution against constituted authority, or treason,
became a capital offense.   The people made this decision;
no one else.   However, they could not possibly have meant
to give the monarch the right to do what the Torah binds him
not to do.   Thus, even after the so-called grant of power to
Joshua by the people, the ruler could not order anyone to do
what was in violation of the Law, nor could he violate the
Law himself.   The Talmud has a very impressive discussion
of this limitation.   In one Biblical illustration, King Ahab
coveted the vineyard of Naboth.   Naboth refused to part
with his patrimony.   Queen Jezebel goaded her husband to
charge Naboth with cursing God and the king, whereupon
Naboth was executed and his property was confiscated.
Mind you, for cursing the king alone no death penalty would
have ensued.   Ahab had to add the charge that God too was
cursed.   However, Elijah denounced the king with the
immortal words "Did you commit murder and then become
your victim's heir?"   This story encapsulates two fundamental views of Judaism--no monarch is above the Law and
no human being may profit by his own wrong.
     The notion that there are limitations on all who
exercise authority is so pervasive in Jewish thought that in
the Middle Ages the Torah was the basis for denying even a
majority of the community the power to deprive the
minority of their rights--even their right not to be forced to
bear an unreasonable share of the community's tax burden.
When a ruler orders what is wrongful, one can disobey.   A
Jewish court will uphold the disobedience.   This is a just
rebellion.   The right to rebel is thus safeguarded by the
Jewish legal order when the ruler breaks the Law, or orders

others to do so. From sources that exist in Jewish literature, one would have expected Christian theologians of the first millenium to have been less tolerant of the tyrants of their day. Why they preached unswerving obedience may have been due to many factors. However, in the later Middle Ages, and on the threshold of the modern period, the Bible became the inspiration for all who sought to end tyranny and injustice. But before the 12th century this was not generally accepted.

In this connection one might do well to remember that during that same period Christian theologians were all too willing to reconcile themselves to the institution of slavery, which Jewish law frowned upon. Christian theologians preferred the Aristotelian notion that slavery was natural, or the Stoic perspective that slavery of the soul could not be achieved and therefore slavery of the body did not matter, or the Augustinian view that slavery was punishment for sin. One cannot fault people who have the courage to defy constituted authority when that authority acts or gives orders which offend the constitution, a higher law, or what is generally accepted to be right and proper. This is the Jewish view, and most revolutions prior to those of this century were of that type. The rebels against the British, therefore, were properly designated as "freedom fighters."

Freedom fighters, however, are also subject to the Law—the same higher law in whose name they want to overthrow constituted authority. And here too Judaism makes a point. If one resorts to violence then the violence must be within the parameters of justice, precisely as the cause for one's rebellion must be just. Terrorists differ from freedom fighters because they respect no such limitation. The most eloquent example one can cite of terrorist activity which was as foul as it was pointless was the murder of Israeli athletes in the Munich Olympics some years ago. It would take more genius than either Lenin or Mao had to link the murders with a just purpose. It was not the murder of a tyrant; it was not the overthrow of constituted authority; it was just terror.

With regard to violence, Judaism appears to agree with Konrad Lorenz, that to act with aggression is human. However, as with all instincts, whether the instinct is for food, sex, or recognition, Jewish law never seeks totally to repress, only to control, to regulate, to make constructive, to dignify, even to sanctify. That applies to the drive for violence or aggression as well. For this reason it must be conceded that Judaism is not committed to pacifism. It may be that there were rabbis in the 3d or 4th century who opposed violence as a means of ensuring Jewish survival, but theirs was decidedly a minority point of view. On the other hand, Rabbi Maurice Lamm, in his essay, *Red or Dead*, shows that his sources would establish that pacifism is not a Jewish ideal. If pacifism is the pursuit of peace at any cost, then it is not and never was an authoritative Jewish teaching. Tolstoy rejected all violent resistance to evil in the social order, regardless of cause and circumstance, because an active revolution must fight evil with another evil, namely violence. He believed in passive, individual resistance and derived it from Matthew in the New Testament: "Resist no evil." Gandhi also made passive resistance a strategy of politics and later attempted to make it a policy of state. Gandhi's proposal for Jews during the Holocaust was also passive resistance. Gandhi's passive resistance might have been effective against an England which had a conscience, but was powerless against Hitler. Quite the contrary, it was precisely what Hitler would have wanted.

Even in situations in which humans less beastly than Hitler are the enemy, passive resistance often has serious limitations. It either cannot be consistently maintained, or it results in the loss of the best manpower that a cause can possibly mobilize. One such situation in modern times is that of the Student Non-Violent Coordinating Committee, which played an important role in the black revolution in the United States during the sixties. Howard Zinn's *The New Abolitionists* questions how nonviolent direct action can be, and he proves, for example, that in 1964 the group had to concede that it would not stop a black farmer in Mississippi from arming himself to defend his home against attack.

Judaism, therefore, is more concerned with regulating the circumstances which would permit the exercise of violence by individuals, by groups, or by states than it is with the elimination of violence at all costs. Violence is at one and the same time an important way both to destroy or conserve one of the most important values in the value system of Judaism: human life. Violent action usually endangers the life of the aggressor as well as the lives of those against whom the violence is directed. Generally one's own life is regarded as having the highest priority, but if one is to engage in violence it must be in accord with Jewish law and in behalf of the value of life or a value even higher than the value of life. Never is one to lose sight of the ultimate value to be achieved. Thus, war for war's sake, which in Judaism is represented by Amalek, is the essence of evil. There can be no compromise in opposition to such a policy. Dueling to vindicate one's honor is heinously sinful. Sadism and masochism are not to be tolerated. Even asceticism is frowned upon in that it is held to be a form of violence against the self, execpt in the very special case where nothing less will help one to overcome physically or spiritually destructive behavior. It is obvious that when one practices violence against an aggressor to save one's own life, one is committed to a value--the value of one's own life. One has a right to prefer one's own life to the life of the attacker. However, may one use an innocent bystander to protect oneself? Or may one kill another pursuant to the request of the attacker in order to save one's own life? Jewish law in such cases says that it is morally wrong to do this, although one may not be punished for so doing except by God Himself.

Jewish law also held that if an enemy should demand that a city surrender to it one person--male or female--or face total destruction, it is better that all should die rather than save themselves by betraying an innocent human being. In Jewish history communities may have been saved by volunteers who martyred themselves, but to use the life of an innocent person for any purpose was absolutely forbidden, even if the purpose is to save many lives.

Are modern day terrorists guided by such an ethic?   I
refer especially to terrorists who are killing their own
people; and not even enemies.   They have no regard
whatever for human life.   And when they are trained by a
foreign state to infiltrate into another country to destroy
it, they certainly are not guided by any regard for the value
of human life.   What was so remarkable about the
underground activity of Jews in Palestine before the
establishment of the State of Israel was that they attacked
principally military objectives, never civilians, and only
rarely the military personnel of Britain.   They were
mindful of the sanctity of human life.   How can one equate
them with the terrorists of today!   During the Holocaust
many Jews suffered martyrdom because they would not
substitute someone else for themselves on the lists marked
for the gas chambers.   And it happened in Jewish history
that many a community refused to resist and kill Christian
attackers because of the disastrous effect their resistance
would have on Jews elsewhere.

A Muslim minority in a Christian country could always
threaten assailants with reprisals against the Christian
minorities in lands where Muslims were the majority.   Jews,
however, even when they were in a position to deal a strong
blow, found that they had to subordinate the destiny of their
particular community to the welfare of Jews all over the
world.   Thus, for example, the Jews of Tulczyn in 1648
refrained from attacking treacherous fellow combatants
among the noblemen.   They chose to die instead when their
leaders exhorted them: "We are in exile among the
nations.   If you lay hands upon the nobles, then all the
kings of Christianity will hear of it and take revenge on all
our brethren in the dispersion, God Forbid."   In our own
century we had a tragic but eloquent example of what the
Jews always dreaded.   I refer to the bullet fired in 1938 by
Herschel Grynszpan.   At that time Poland was calling back
all of her citizens, and Herschel Grynszpan's parents were
caught in a vise.   After receiving a letter from his parents
describing their distress, he decided to take revenge by
destroying some great Nazi officials.   He crept into an
embassy in Paris and killed a third-rate bureaucrat of

Nazidom. That shot was the pretext for the dreadful pogrom of November 1938, which precipitated a reprisal against all the Jews in Germany.

Is the situation so different today? Self-defense may sometimes be helpful to one Jewish community, but Jews must always be terribly concerned about how it will affect Jewish communities elsewhere. Thus Jews in South Africa are concerned when the State of Israel exercises its sovereign rights to vote in the United Nations in accordance with the dictates of its conscience against South Africa. And the Jews of the Soviet Union are hostages in order to force Jews in the United States not to be too militant in support of a Jackson Amendment.

From all of this it appears that even in self-defense one must be mindful of values, even in self-defense there is no absolute right to engage in violence. Thus, while Jewish law does not absolutely outlaw the right to rebel or resort to violence, it is preoccupied with the when, where, and how. Perhaps this should apply to all rights.

CHAPTER II

Terrorists or
Freedom Fighters

Professor M. Arens

I visited Lebanon recently and two of the Lebanese Moslems I met in separate places (one spoke good English and the other spoke through an interpreter) said to me: "You know we were in America during the Israeli invasion of Lebanon" (and they used that expression), "and your appearances on television were just terrific. You really described it as it was." But, just to show that there is always another side to the coin, a newspaper which likes to think that it is the Israeli *New York Times*, ran an article while I was ambassador in the United States during the "Peace for Galilee Operation" about the Israeli information effort in the United States at the time. The reporter said: "Of all the people who are trying to explain Israel's case in the U.S., the worst of all is our ambassador." So, there are two sides to every coin.

The title, "Terrorists or Freedom Fighters" is a sign of the times that should be a source for discussions and I suppose probably a difference of opinions stemming from the general feeling of ambiguity that is felt throughout the world on this subject. George Orwell's predictions really have not come true; things don't look like they did in his book *1984*. Nevertheless, there are certain things and characteristics of the times that we live in that we can associate with his book. "Double think" and "double speak" certainly occur in our day and age, not only in communist societies, but likewise in western societies.

The fact that terrorists and terrorist leaders are labelled and accepted by many as freedom fighters is really nothing less than *1984*. Is it at all reasonable or logical to think of Yasir Arafat as a modern day Garibaldi, or George Habbash as a 1984 Masaryk? Freedom fighting is the antithesis of what these people are doing, have done, and want to do--the very antithesis of freedom fighters as we know them. And yet I think there is no question but that Yasir Arafat and George Habbash have not succeeded in the Soviet Union or in East Germany but they have succeeded in convincing a large number of people in the Western world-- some members of Jewish communities, some members of the Israeli public--that they are legitimate freedom fighters and that they have a legitimate grievance. All you have to do is satisfy their grievance and they will lay down their arms in the tradition of freedom fighters in other ages.

Israel has had the poor fortune of having to contend with terrorism more than any other country in the world. And I suppose one reason for this is that we are located in the Middle East. All Middle Eastern peoples have had to contend and are contending with terrorism in very large measure. The whole Middle East has an ongoing history-- not only Israel, or Palestine before Israel was established-- of people being killed in large numbers to serve political purposes. The scene where terrorism has been focused more than any other place in the past years has been Lebanon. We clearly see acts of terrorism perpetrated there to destabilze the government, to bring the government down, and to bring chaos to the area, without any regard to the well being of the people who live in the country.

Look at the list of recent terrorist acts in Lebanon and terrorism is taking place in Lebanon at this very moment, day in, day out. There was the assassination of Beshir Gemayel, the President-elect of Lebanon, we know whose purposes that was supposed to serve. It is impossible to reconcile that act with any freedom movement of any sort.

There was the bombing of the U.S. Embassy in Beirut.   It is impossible to reconcile that with freedom movements, as we understand them.   There were a number of attempted assassinations of Lebanese personalities, and there was the car-bombing of the Marine compound and the simultaneous car-bombing of the French compound in Beirut.   There was a car-bombing of an Israeli installation in Tyre, the abduction of Professor Dodd, the President of the American University in Beirut, the assassination of Professor Kerr, President of the University in Beirut, to recall a few of the more significant terrorist acts.

This is just a run-down of a series of terrorist acts committed in Lebanon recently that take their place in the long line of terrorist acts that go back to Avivim and Maalot.   Israelis, I'm sure, know what I am talking about, some of the people from farther afield may have forgotten what that means; the Olympic Games in Munich and many others.

I think that what is significant about terrorism as it is practiced in the present is something that has been pointed out by President Reagan not so long ago.   It is something we have discussed with the United States on a government-to-government level this past year or two: much of this terrorism--I think all the terrorist acts that I have alluded to in Lebanon--are state supported.   These are not just a group of terrorists who happen to get their hands on some dynamite, or some Kalashmikov rifles.   These are terrorist groups that are operating under government cover with government   support--in   effect   under   government sponsorship.   And government support is what makes them so dangerous and is what makes them so effective because it provides a dimension of capability for them that small groups of terrorists could never obtain.   They can train on open training grounds--not underground--in the Soviet Union, South Yemen, Syria, Libya, or in Iraq.   These terrorists can send their rifles and dynamite through diplomatic pouches, and they do. They can hide in embassies.   They are simply another arm of some states who practice terrorism.

We have four such states in this area. I think they can correctly be called four "crazy" states in the sense that they behave completely different than states in Western society. These are Khomeini's Iran, Assad's Syria, Saddam Hussein's Iraq, and Qaddafi's Libya. These are four "crazy" states. All four of these states practice terrorism and provide government cover through their embassies, through their diplomatic pouches, and using military equipment from their armed forces for terrorist movements. You may have noted that Jordanian diplomats have been slain in various parts of the world. There is no question that they are being killed by terrorists who are sent by the Syrian government. The list of terrorist acts in Lebanon mentioned previously is the result of Syrian sponsorship and, in some cases, Syrian-Iranian cooperation. That Qaddafi sends out death-squads throughout the world is no secret.

I think that it is important to recognize that these terrorist acts frequently are effective, not only in killing the intended target, but in having much wider repercussions. And I think it is that realization that should bring us all and the non-crazy governments in the world to the resolution that we have to work in concert in order to contend with this very real danger to peoples throughout the world. In Lebanon I have seen the effects of this terrorism. It is the effect that is intended by the terrorists. I think it would be fair to say that the majority of Lebanese spanning all ethnic and religious denominations--Christians, Druse, Shi'ite, and Sunni--harbor no enmity to Israel. Quite the contrary, they look to Israel to provide some degree of stability and assistance on the road to normalcy in that tragedy-ridden land. I say the majority. It is an understatement. There is hardly a Lebanese whom I have met who has not expressed these feelings to me. Lately there is hardly a Lebanese whom I meet who does not plead and implore me--as Israeli's Minister of Defense--not to evacuate any additional areas of Lebanon. There was no Lebanese in the Shute area before the Israel Defense Forces left that area who did not plead with me to delay the evacuation. A significant majority of Lebanese look to Israel not with enmity but with friendship. They look to

Israel as a factor in the area that can be helpful in keeping
their country from being subjugated again by the Syrians
and putting an end to those years of turmoil, terror, and
killing.

The terrorist activities in Lebanon sponsored and
directed by some of the "crazy" states--the Syrians, to
some extent, and the Iranians, more so lately--is directed
at stilling these voices. Their activities have been
reasonably successful. If you follow the media, you will
not get the impression of the true feeling of the people of
Lebanon. Thus, the people who throw the bombs, who kill
the people, are gaining the effect that they seek, or at least
they see progress toward their ultimate objective. We will
do whatever we can to make sure that they don't.

We have had a similar phenomenon in Judea and
Samaria. I suppose that most people in the world at the
present have the impression that all of the Palestinian
population in these areas are opposed to Israel presence--to
Israel's occupation, as it is frequently described--and are
ready to participate in the struggle for national liberation
in order to remove the Israeli presence from these areas.
We have not taken any public opinion polls in the area. I
do not know that this is really possible in the sense that
public opinion polls are taken in the Western world. But
since becoming Israel's Minister of Defense, I have spent
some of my time talking to people in Judea and Samaria.
Israel's military operations and the PLO defeat in
Lebanon, have had a very far-ranging effect on the feelings
or ability of people in Judea and Samaria to express their
feelings. Now I hear things that I would not have heard
some years ago because of the fear of terrorist activities.
The list of Palestinian leaders in Judea, Samaria, and Gaza
who have been killed by PLO terrorists is a long one. Just
about every person in Judea and Samaria whom I have
visited recently tells me that they do not support the PLO.
They realize that terrorism is no way to accomplish any kind
of objective in the area. Terrorism can not bring about a
resolution of the outstanding problems in the area. The
first priority for Jews and Arabs is learning to live together
in peace. If people can permit themselves to say that to

me it is because in some sense they feel that they have been liberated from the yoke of terrorism. They feel they do not have to fear an attack after a meeting with me. This experience shows that terrorism can be fought successfully. It also shows how negative the consequences can be if we're not successful in fighting terrorism.

I'm glad to see that today in the United States, in the Reagan administration there is a recognition of the danger of terrorism, especially of the danger of state supported terrorism. I'm hopeful that that recognition will be felt in other democratic countries. I think if we have not been more successful in fighting terrorism than we have been these past years, it is because Israel has stood almost alone in it's fight against terrorism. If the democratic countries in the world band together, take the appropriate action, not only against terrorists in individual cases but against those states who support terrorism, if they tear away from them the mask of legitimacy, and if they refuse to carry on proper diplomatic relations with countries that sponsor and support terrorism, I think that we will go a long way towards destroying terrorism and its very negative effects throughout the world.

PART TWO
INTERNATIONAL PERSPECTIVE

CHAPTER III

State Sponsored Terrorism

Ray S. Cline
Yonah Alexander

The semantic confusion over the precise definition of terrorism, particularly the subset of the species that can be identified as state-sponsored, has hindered formulation of national and military policy by nations of the free world. Consequently, it has been hard to formulate authoritative and systematic doctrinal and policy recommendations on initiatives to prevent, deter, and decrease the effectiveness of terrorist acts, or to punish identified terrorists after the fact.

The general uncertainty over what constitutes terrorism is linked to a proliferation of terms dealing with the entire spectrum of conflict below the level of what is traditionally perceived as an internationally recognized state of organized war.[1] Each agency or office of government has approached the problem of definition from its own point of view and responsibilities. Only now is opinion in the United States beginning to crystallize in a way that permits a serious attempt to form a consensus on this menacing phenomenon.

BASIC ELEMENTS OF AN ANATOMY OF TERRORISM

An analysis of the most carefully phrased definitions indicates that an effective definition must deal with the following components or elements of terrorism:

- **Nature of the Act**: The concept embraces violence or threat of violence, other criminal, unlawful, politically subversive, or anarchic acts; piracy; hijacking of aircraft; and taking of hostages.
- **Perpetrators**: States must to be identified as perpetrators, along with individuals and private groups; clearly, states sponsoring terrorism are the chief international troublemakers today.
- **Strategic Objectives**: Certain states sponsor terrorism as part of a campaign of geographic expansion of political control by one-party dictatorships at the expense of existing state structures based on political pluralism and representative government. A striking shortcoming in current definitions is that no mention is made of this important variable of the 1980s.
- **Intended Outcome**: Fear, extortion, and radical political change are most often the expected results.
- **Targets**: Human beings and property are specific targets of terrorist acts, with special focus on heads of state, diplomats, and public officials. Military targets should be included because soldiers in non-combat or peacekeeping roles are often primary victims.
- **Methods**: Threats, as well as the actual resort to sabotage, hostage-taking, murder, kidnapping, and bombing (including letter or parcel bombing) involving the use of automatic weapons, grenades, and rockets are common methods of terrorists in spreading fear among targeted populations; weapons of mass destruction cannot be excluded.

INTERGOVERNMENTAL DEFINITIONS

Historically, the earliest treatments of the definition of terrorism in this century are in treaties between states that have defined specific actions appropriate to deal with specific crimes, e.g., piracy or the taking of hostages.2　In the Convention for the Prevention and Punishment of Terrorism (Geneva, November 16, 1937), 23 signatories defined terrorism as "Criminal acts directed against a state and intended or calculated to create a state of terror in the minds of particular persons, or a group of persons, or the general public."3　On the same date in conjunction with this treaty, the League of Nations drafted a parallel Convention for the Creation of an International Criminal Court to make "progress in the struggle against offenses of an international character."4　Although this instrument never entered into force, it was the first international attempt to establish judicial machinery to deal with the offense of terrorism as defined by the League in a time of increasing violence. The collapse of the League and the advent of World War II, of course, brought all of this early 20th century thinking to naught.　After World War II and especially in the last two or three decades, terrorism has once again spread widely.　It occurs frequently with more and more disastrous results, but attempts to progress beyond the abortive international efforts made in 1937 have so far also failed.

When Secretary-General Kurt Waldheim of the United Nations initiated discussion of a policy on international terrorism promoted by the growing number of incidents as long ago as 1972, he did not anticipate the depth and intensity of the Third World's resistance to efforts to define terrorist offenses as crimes.　Instead, he was forced to change his central focus from terrorist acts themselves to the misery, frustration, and grievances allegedly giving rise to these acts.　This focus seemed to imply tolerance or even justification of terrorism.　While the United Nations has not succeeded since that time in its attempts to provide a global concensus on the meaning of terrorism, it has been more effective in identifying some specific offenses and in

taking some juridical steps to cope with them. This was
the case when major nations shared a common concern over
the danger. These offenses are set forth in An International Convention Against the Taking of Hostages drafted
by the General Assembly and signed in 1978.[5]
    Several of the U.N. specialized agencies have concen-
trated on categories of terrorist activities directly related
to their mandates. In 1963, they dealt with the unlawful
seizure of aircraft;[6] in 1971, they covered the offenses of
sabotage;[7] in 1974, they passed an article prohibiting
explosive, flammable, or other dangerous substances in
letters;[8] and in 1979, they categorized as criminal offenses
acts involving the theft of or threatened usage of nuclear
material to cause death or serious injury.[9] Following
endorsement by the General Assembly of the Organization
of American States (OAS) on June 30, 1970,[10] of efforts to
prevent and punish acts of terrorism and a similar resolution
by the Council of Europe on January 27, 1977,[11] many
member states of these organizations signed conventions
urging effective measures for the suppression of terrorist
crimes like kidnapping, extortion, or attack against life or
liberty of internationally protected persons, including
diplomatic agents. The problem facing the intergovernmental organizations is not the availability of substantial
conceptual elements of international law condemning
particular aspects of terrorism, but the vagueness and
confusion about the implementation, enforcement, or
interpretation of the law.

ATTEMPTS BY FOREIGN GOVERNMENTS
TO DEFINE TERRORISM

    The definitional focus of each sovereign government
depends first and foremost on the nature of its internal and
external policies. Every sovereign state reserves to itself
the political and legal authority to determine what is and
what is not terrorism in the context of domestic and foreign
affairs. For instance, the United Kingdom applies the term
to the Irish Republican Army, and Israel regards all PLO
acts as terrorist. Certain states have complicated the

definition of the nature of terrorism by dealing with it solely as a part of their own politically motivated psychological warfare and propaganda. A case in point is the exploitation of the terms "liberation struggle" or "war of national liberation" by the Soviet Union as a defense against criticism by the United States of Soviet-sponsored terrorist acts.

For instance, on April 27, 1981, welcoming Libya's Colonel Qadhafi to Moscow as a "comrade in the struggle for the rights and freedoms of peoples," President Brezhnev scornfully repudiated the critical views of the United States of Qadhafi, saying "Imperialists have no regard either for the will of the people or the laws of history. Liberation struggles cause their indignation. They describe them as 'terrorism.'"[12] Similarly, Marshal Dimitri Ustinov, until his recent death a Member of the Politburo of the Soviet Communist Party and Minister of Defense, defined terrorism as the actions of "neofascism." He further pointed out that the "evil-minded" charges against Moscow were intended to "cover up Western subversion of Poland and other countries." In general, Ustinov concluded, terrorism is "one of the most terrible manifestations of the moral and political crisis of capitalist society and the embodiment of lawlessness."[13] From these statements it is not hard to understand how the USSR opened up all its propaganda outlets to blame the United States for allegedly assassinating Prime Minister Indira Gandhi in October 1984. There was no shred of evidence to support this ridiculous allegation, but Moscow sought to muddy the waters of international opinion by trumped-up charges. The concept of Moscow and Washington on these matters are cultural worlds apart. The Soviet Union has only defined specific acts as terrorism, such as hijacking, when its own interests are at stake. Thus, the USSR signed bilateral treaties on the hijacking of aircraft with Afghanistan (1971), Iran (1973), and Finland (1974).[14] Similarly, Cuba also entered into bilateral agreements on hijacking with the United States (1973),[15] Canada (1973),[16] Mexico (1973),[17] and Colombia (1974).[18]

Nations in the free world have recognized a need to define a wider range of acts of terrorism in order to determine their policy goals. Each one concentrates on its particular experience to relate them to its choice of terminology. Argentina calls terrorism a "flagrant violation of human rights ... (and) incompatible with the concept of human dignity."[19] France states terrorism is a "heinous act of barbarism."[20] Venezuela emphasizes that it is any act that "endangers or takes innocent human lives, or jeopardizes fundamental freedoms."[21]

U.S. PERCEPTIONS OF TERRORISM

The United States as a pluralist democracy speaks with a bewildering variety of voices on the subject of terrorism. The vast literature accumulating throughout the U.S. Government and the private sector reveals that terrorism has countless causes, forms, and effects. It is ancient, it is pervasive although cyclical in intensity, and it is plainly on a very high plateau after a rising trend over the past 20 years. The vagueness in the American public consciousness about its character and meaning is due to the diverse and protean forms and alleged purposes of the terrorist act itself, as well as to official and unofficial disagreements concerning its nature, scope, and appropriate responses. The prevailing tendency has been to view each terrorist act as an individual incident without political pattern or strategic dimension. This attitude is naive in view of the accumulating evidence of collusion among states sponsoring violence against pluralist democracies, particularly the United States and its allies abroad.

When all the definitions and legislative formulas have been reviewed, the elements of commonality bring one back to the normal usages of careful students of the English language. The Oxford Dictionary includes primary meanings of terrorism:

> First, it is government by intimidation as directed and carried out by the party in power in France during the revolution of 1789-1794: the system of terror (1793-1794).

Second, it connotes a policy intended to strike with terror those against whom it is adopted; the employment of methods of intimidation; the fact of terrorizing.

The first meaning is exactly what should be called state terrorism, as practiced by Lenin, Stalin, and Mao. The second meaning is broader, embracing "employment of methods of intimidation" by any individual or group. When a state supports or encourages "the fact of terrorizing" by individuals or groups acting outside its own border, the phenomenon is state-sponsored terrorism, a missing element in the standard dictionary. The heart of the problem of the definition is that the use of violence for political purposes, real or hidden, cannot be viewed as value-free. The purposes make the difference. The cultural, moral, and political values of the society that has evolved in the United States during 200 years of constitutionalism and representative government must enter into the official American working definition of this troublesome phenomenon. Officials and military services must reflect the basic standards of American citizens' judgments about the aim of terrorists to determine what it is and whether it is culpable.

Terrorism is obviously perceived differently by perpetrators, victims, and observers. To the attackers, "whoever stands by a just cause cannot possibly be called a terrorist."[22] On the other hand, the diverse origins and semantic justifications of this sort of act are irrelevant to the victims. The unaffected observer determines the pejorative or favorable view of the act from the political perspective of the ultimate international results.

Here the United States must take a principled stand on the high ground of devotion to the defense of freedom. Self-defense is a legitimate posture in the defense of society and institutions as well as individual human beings. Americans should make the most of this fact. History bears out that terrorism begets more terrorism, usually resulting in diminished freedom and restricted human rights unless firm and well-defined defensive measures are taken. In the context of Soviet strategic aims and conduct of

Soviet client states, terrorist activity of the kind Moscow
labels "wars of national liberation" leads to political
oppression and tyranny, not to the improvement of society.
Unless Americans see this clearly, it will be impossible to
cope with the dark impulses of the legacy of Yuri Andropov.
This fact is why it is imperative to define terrorism of the
1980s in its full strategic dimension, reflecting its
geopolitical purpose.

LACK OF CONSENSUS IN NON-GOVERNMENTAL DEFINITIONS

Expert writers or spokesmen, working in the media or in
academe, have not produced a uniform working definition of
terrorism.   In fact, the proliferation of definitions in these
fields underscores the diversity of attitudes.   The problem
is compounded by the fact that the free media in democratic
societies are based on competition and profit.   They see
terrorism as attention-grabbing news and seldom worry
about consistency of categorization.   It is inevitable, in
view of the terrorist search for publicity, that the media
become an integral part of the terrorist act.   Describing
this phenomenon, Ford Rowan, host of the International
Edition, Independent Network News, observed, "Terrorism
is an act of theater and, unfortunately, the media are its
stage.   The press, and especially the electronic media,
seem to thrive on the sensational.   The terrorists for their
part, manufacture sensations to capture the attention of the
fascinated public."[23]
Similarly, articulation by academics and experts in the
United States of what is and is not terrorism has been so
disorganized and diverse that it has left us in a kind of
intellectual and moral limbo.   As Secretary of State
George Shultz said of the difficulty of responding
adequately to the terrorist threat, the United States risks
becoming a "Hamlet of nations."[24]   Indeed, a survey of the
literature illustrates the difficulty in determining scientifi-
cally the nature and meaning of terrorism.   There is a
proliferation of variables connected with the psychological
effects.   They include fear, intimidation, coercion, anxi-

ety, and mental distress. Atribution of motives to terrorists ranges from manipulating psychological attitudes to committing genocide. Only a handful of writers speak of political or strategic objectives based on competing social and political values leading to terrorist crimes.

THE U.S. FEDERAL SYSTEM

Under the U.S. federal system, each state determines what constitutes an offense under its criminal or penal code. An increasing number of states has defined terrorism generically as a crime, thus evading the use of specific statutes covering selected criminal acts identified as terrorism. These state laws characteristically deal with criminality of particular acts of violence but not with sponsorship by foreign nations nor military aspects of the problem.

A typical example of state statutes is the Arkansas Criminal Code. It declares:

> A person commits the offense of terroristic threatening if with the purpose of terrorizing another person he threatenes to cause death or serious physical injury or substantial property damage to another person.
> ... a person commits a terroristic act when, while not in the commission of a lawful act, he shoots at or in any manner projects an object with the intent to cause injury to persons or property at a conveyance which is being operated or which is occupied with passengers.[25]

Since state statutes focus only on domestic expressions of terrorism, it is the mandate of the U.S. Congress to define state-sponsored terrorism.

ROLE OF THE U.S. CONGRESS

The conceptual effort to define the meaning and nature of terrorism and its relation to the whole spectrum of conflict has in fact in recent years engaged the attention of

the U.S. Congress.   Congress has over several years held
hearings, considered more than 70 bills, adopted resolutions,
and passed laws on terrorism.   "Nevertheless, a comprehensive working definition that can address the different
forms of terrorist activity has not emerged from the
Congress thus far.

A case in point of a very serious approach to the
subject is Senate bill S.2236 of 1977 aimed "to strengthen
federal policies and programs and international cooperation
to combat international terrorism."   Senator Abraham
Ribicoff, Chairman of the Committee on Governmental
Affairs, introduced the bill, known as An Act to Combat
International Terrorism, in the Senate on October 25, 1977.
The bill's definition included the following components:

> **First,** the definition builds on crimes defined under
> certain international conventions.
> **Second,** the definition includes descriptions of the
> other unlawful actions.
> **Third,** the definition concerns itself with the
> place--the international context.
> **Fourth,** the definition provides that to be criminal
> in the context of the bill, such acts must be
> targeted at least in part against the interests of
> state or international organizations.
> **Fifth,** the definition provides that essentially
> military operations are not to be considered acts
> of terrorism.

More comprehensive definitional treatment was offered
along the same lines in the U.S. environment by Senator
Jeremiah Denton, Chairman of the Subcommittee on
Security and Terrorism, Committee of the Judiciary, in his
introduction to the Anti-Terrorism Act of 1984.   He said:

> ... terrorism means the knowing use of force or
> violence against any person or property in
> violation of the criminal laws of the United States
> or any state, territory, possession, or district, with
> the intent to intimidate, coerce, or influence a

government or person in furtherance of any
political or ideological objective.[26]

Despite the enunciation of this broad definition, more
serviceable in these times than most, Senator Denton
himself adopted a narrower approach under different
circumstances of congressional consideration. In the Act
of Rewards for Information Concerning Terrorist Acts (98th
Congress, 2nd Session, H.R. 5612), the senator limited
terrorism to those acts which are intended:

- to intimidate or coerce a civilian population,
- to influence the policy of a government by
  intimidation or coercion, or
- to affect the conduct of a government by
  assassination or kidnapping.

Moreover, Congress has tended to define terrorism
mainly in terms of specific criminal offenses with an
international aspect. The congressional acts include
Crimes Against Internationally Protected Persons,[27] Crimes
Against Aviation,[28] and Crimes Against Taking of
Hostages.[29]

THE EXECUTIVE BRANCH

Numerous working definitions of terrorism are beginning to be formed in the official statements issued by the
executive branch in attempts to define policy in the face of
proliferating terrorist violence. In the late 1970s, statutory definitions encompassed most of the elements typically
incorporated within the category of international terrorism,
but they did not deal with the special problem of state
sponsorship or consider terrorism as a form of international
conflict, e.g., covert warfare. In the 1980s, these two
definitional elements are finally being regularly accepted
by most senior officials.

In 1980, the Central Intelligence Agency specified that
"international terrorism is terrorism conducted with the
support of a foreign government or organization and/or

directed against foreign nationals, institutions, or governments."30 In 1984, Louis O. Giuffrida, Director of the
Federal Emergency Management Agency, stated that "it is
only inevitable that more and more terrorism will be state-
sponsored because it is the cheapest and least hazardous
way to fight an undeclared war."31 It is not surprising
that the Department of Defense, when reporting on the
truck bombing of the U.S. Marine headquarters in Beirut,
emphasized the "unlawful use or threatened use of force or
violence by a revolutionary organization."32 The Department of the Army, although adhering in general to the
"violence" theme, adds, "Terrorism involves a criminal act
that is often symbolic in nature and intended to influence an
audience beyond the immediate victims."33

This linkage between terrorism and psychological
warfare is also underscored by the Department of State, its
officials, and a number of representatives of other
governmental agencies. In June 1984, Ambassador Jeane J.
Kirkpatrick, then U.S. Permanent Representative to the
United Nations, explained emphatically, "Terrorism is a
form of war against a society and all who embody it....
Terrorist war is part of a total war which sees the whole
society as the enemy, and all members of a society as
appropriate objects for violent action."34

Secretary Shultz, who has primary responsibility for
determining the meaning of terrorism for the entire
executive branch, has developed and explained his own
perceptions of terrorism in increasing awareness of the
current techniques of international resort to violence. On
June 24, 1984, he equated terrorism roughly with war and
spoke of the rise of state-sponsorship.35 On October 25,
1984, he called terrorism "a form of political violence" that
is "neither random nor without purpose."36 "But the
overarching goal of all terrorists is the same. They are
trying to impose their will by force--a special kind of force
designed to create an atmosphere of fear ... they want
people to lose faith in their government's capacity to
protect them and thereby to undermine the legitimacy of
the government itself, or its policies, or both. We must
understand, however," he continued, "that terrorism,

wherever it takes place, is directed in an important sense
against us, the democracies--against our most basic values
and often our fundamental strategic interests."[37]   A few
months later, on February 4, 1985, when speaking of defense
against terrorism, Shultz declared, "Terrorism poses a
direct threat not only to Western strategic interests but to
the very moral principles that undergird Western democratic society.   The enemies of the West are united.   So too
must the democratic countries be united in a common
defense against terrorism."[38]

On March 6, 1984, President Reagan sent a package of
four anti-terrorism bills to the Congress designed to deal
with some of the dangers posed by international terrorism.
They included proposed legislation against aircraft sabotage, against the taking of hostages, and against training
and support of terrorist organizations.   The fourth established a reward for information concerning terrorist acts.
In the closing days before the election recess, Congress
passed three of the bills, all except the one calling for
prohibition against training or supporting terrorist organizations.   At the time he submitted these bills, the president
pointed out that over the past decade almost 6,500 terrorist
incidents had taken place and that approximately 40 percent
of these had been targeted against American citizens.   He
deplored the increased emergence of state terrorism, which,
he said, was "starkly manifest in the recent spectacles of
violence in Beirut, Rangoon, and Kuwait.   State-sponsored
terrorists," he continued, "pose a severe challenge to the
conduct of U.S. foreign policy as well as to the security of
U.S. citizens."[39]

This whole legislative exercise was in part an
educational effort to communicate the serious meaning of
terrorism to the Congress and to the American people.

A WORKING U.S. DEFINITION

All U.S. Agencies soon must adopt a final coordinated
position on the meaning of the most complex and
troublesome international danger of the 1980s.   Terrorists
resort to a variety of means to cause conflict or unrest in

the entire ideological, political, social, economic, and
strategic spectrum. Threats and psychological destabilization economic, and strategic spectrum. Physical violence, naturally uppermost in U.S. media and public concern,
is only one of the modes of creating terror. Threats and
psychological destabilization are often equally dangerous to
social stability. The destructive effect of all forms of
terrorist action is obvious both in the damage to social and
political tranquility it causes as well as in the destruction of
lives and property.

The Army's formulation of this phenomenon provides a
reasonable working definition of terrorism. Army Regulation 190-52 states that terrorism is:

> ... the calculated use of violence or the threat of
> violence to attain goals political, religious, or
> ideological in nature. This is done through
> intimidation, coercion, or instilling fear. Terror-
> ism involves a criminal act that is often symbolic
> in nature and effects an audience beyond the
> immediate victims.

From all the foregoing history and analysis, it is
possible to go beyond this formulation to derive a working
definition of state-sponsored terrorism, as a subset of
terrorism. It must reflect American social and political
values and have useful policy and operational benefits for
democratic societies. This definition specifically includes
members of the armed forces, since military service
personnel in non-combat roles are frequently finding
themselves among possible targets. They are seldom
included in current conceptualizations of the phenomenon
of modern terrorism or appropriate responses to it.

It is suggested that state-sponsored terrorism be
defined as:

> The deliberate employment of violence or the
> threat of use of violence by sovereign states (or
> sub-national groups encouraged or assisted by
> sovereign states) to attain strategic and political
> objectives by acts in violation of law intended to
> create overwhelming fear in a target population

larger than the civilian or military victims attacked or threatened.

It is further suggested that recent history indicates:

The main goal of this state-sponsored terrorism now at the end of the 20th century is to undermine selectively the policies, the psychosocial stability, and political governability of pluralist states with representative governments.

This somewhat cumbersome but carefully crafted two-part definition has many advantages over most other formulations in current use. Not the least of its virtues is that it reflects the spirit of the attitudes of serious-minded American citizens as well as the recent policy positions voiced by President Reagan and Secretary Shultz. In international affairs legal concepts are seldom juristically value-free since 170 sovereign nations make their own laws governing their own practices and policies. It is crucial for the United States to employ a realistic definition of terrorism that effectively deals with the international behavior actually being encountered today and that also makes sense in the context of the American political culture.

This working definition of state-sponsored terrorism meets the following criteria while systematically describing the main elements in the earlier outlined anatomy of terrorism.

- An act of violence, whether threatened or carried out, is criminal and terroristic if it is in violation of national or international law and if it is aggressive rather than in defense of a legitimate political order.
- A political organization exercising sovereign powers, whether a nation-state or an organization claiming sovereignty (such as the Palestine Liberation Organization) must be among the perpetrators or must be actively encouraging or directly

supporting the perpetrators of acts of violence in
another country.   Only then is terroristic behavior
identified   as   fitting   the   pattern   of   state--
sponsorship.

● Various political goals may be claimed for terrorists
acts but from the viewpoint of national security
interests of the United States, the classical case of
state-sponsored terrorism is one where the strategic consequence will be major enhancement of the
power of an ideologically totalitarian regime or the
serious weakening of a state structure attempting
to establish or maintain pluralist representative
government.

● The outcome of state-sponsored terrorism must
include creating overwhelming fear in a broad
population being targeted for radical psychological,
social, political, and, hence, strategic change.

● It should be understood that the targets of violence
within the threatened population targeted for
change include military forces on non-combat or
peacekeeping missions as well as officials and
businessmen.

● Any methods employing or threatening violent
attacks against human beings or state and private
property qualify as an act of terrorism and if the
perpetrators include sovereign political organiza-
tions--as state-sponsored terrorism.

The anatomy of modern politically and ideologically
oriented acts of violence involving sovereign states is
better outlined in the suggested working definition
presented here than in any other commonly used definition.
It should be considered for adoption by the armed services
and the U.S. Government as whole.

NOTES

1.   This analysis is based on a comprehensive survey of
several hundred definitions utilized by governmental,

intergovernmental, and non-governmental organizations, the media, and the academic community. During September-December 1984, the authors of this work sent out a questionnaire to gather this information.

2.   The first treaty is called "Treaty for the Extradition of Criminals and for the Protection Against Anarchism," Mexico City, January 28, 1902.   The signatories were the Argentine Republic, Bolivia, Colombia, Costa Rica, Chile, the Dominican Republic, Ecuador, El Salvador, the United States, Guatemala, Haiti, Honduras, the United Mexican States, Nicaragua, Paraguay, Peru, and Uruguay.   Yonah Alexander, Marjorie Ann Browne, and Allan S. Nanes, eds., *Control of Terrorism: International Documents*, New York: Crane Russak, 1979, pp 3-9.

3.   *Ibid.*, pp 19-29.

4.   *Ibid.*, pp 31-42.

5.   U.N. General Assembly, 33rd Session, Sixth Committee, Agenda Item 120, A/C.6/33/L.6, November 15, 1978.

6.   20 UST 2941; TIAS 6768; entered into force December 4, 1969.

7.   24 UST 564; TIAS 7570; entered into force January 26, 1973.

8.   UKTS, No 57 (1976), Cmnd. 6538; in force since January 1, 1976.

9.   Brian M. Jenkins, "International Cooperation in Locating and Recovering Stolen Nuclear Materials," *Terrorism: An International Journal*, V 6, No 4 (1983), p 572.

10. TIAS 8481.

11. Dur. T.S., No 90 and Great Britain.   Papers by Command Condor: Her Majesty's Stationary, 1977.   (Cmnd. 7031).

12. *Washington Post* and *New York Times*, April 28, 1981. Cited in Ray S. Cline and Yonah Alexander, *Terrorism: The Soviet Connection*, New York: Crane Russak, 1984, p 22.

13. *Strategic Review*, V I, Spring 1981, p 9.   Cited in Cline and Alexander.   *Op. cit.*, pp 22-23.

14. Alona Evans and John Murphy, eds., *Legal Aspects of International Terrorism*, Lexington, Mass.:   Lexington Books, 1978, p 48, n 119.

15. 24 UST 737; TIAS 7579.   This agreement was denounced by Cuba in October 1976, in effect from April 15, 1977 (for alleged complicity in sabotage for a Cuban aircraft).

16. Canada Treaty Series, 1973, No 11.

17. *Terrorism: An International Journal*, V 7, No 2 (1984), p 145.

18. *Ibid*.

19. Terrorism in Argentina (a document prepared by the Argentine Government addressed to the Argentine people), January 7, 1970, p 12.

20. See *Report of the Ad Hoc Committee on International Terrorism*, U.N. General Assembly, 28th Session, Supplement No 28 (A/9028), New York, 1973, p 350.

21. *Ibid.*, p 352.

22. Yasser Arafat at the U.N. General Assembly, 1974, quoted by Secretary of State George Shultz before the Park Avenue Synagogue, New York, October 25, 1984.

23. Leonard Theberge and Yonah Alexander, eds., "Terrorism and the Media in the 1980s," (Conference Report), *Political Communication and Persuasion: An International Journal*, V 2, No 3 (1984), p 300.

24. Secretary Shultz, before the Park Avenue Synagogue, New York, October 25, 1984, p 6.

25. Arkansas Criminal Code, Title 41, Section 41-16508 and Title 41, Section 41-1651.

26. *Congressional Record*, V 130, No 35 (March 22, 1984), p 2.

27. Public Law 92-539, October 24, 1972, amended the Criminal Code (Title 18, U.S.C.).

28. Public Law 93-366, August 5, 1974.

29. Public Law 98-473, October 10, 1984.

30. "Pattern of International Terrorism: 1980," a research paper prepared by the National Foreign Assessment Center, Washington, D.C. p ii.   (This is a Central Intelligence Agency publication and is based on information available as of December 31, 1980).

31. "How Can Terrorism Be Stopped?   The Domestic Front," remarks before the Jonathan Institute's Second Conference on International Terrorism, Washington, D.C., June 26, 1984, pp 2, 5.

32. Report of the Department of Defense Commission on Beirut International Airport Terrorist Act, October 23, 1983 (December 20, 1983), p 122.
33. Army Regulation 190-52.
34. Kirkpatrick address before the Jonathan Institute's Second Conference on International Terrorism, Washington, D.C., June 24, 1984, p 2.
35. Kirkpatrick, p 1.
36. Secretary Schultz, Park Avenue Synagogue, New York, October 25, 1984, p 1.
37. Shultz, pp 1-2.
38. Address by Secretary Schultz before the American Society for Industrial Security, Arlington, Virginia, February 4, 1984, p 2.
39. American Bar Association, Standing Committee, *Law and National Security Intelligence Report*, V 6, No 7, July 1984 and V 6, No 11, November 1984.

Note: This chapter was up-dated before going to press.

CHAPTER IV

International Terrorism
and UN Responses

Dr. A. Gerson

The harrowing events in the Middle East--the bombing of the civilian bus in Jerusalem on December 6, 1984, which resulted, among other deaths and maimings, in the loss of the lives of two young sisters, Esther, aged 16, and Nurit, aged 14; the car bombing attacks against multinational peacekeeping forces in Lebanon; the dastardly murder on January 18, 1984, of Malcolm Kerr, President of the American University in Beirut; the increased attacks on diplomatic personnel of many different countries; the explosion of an Air France 747 out of Karachi; and the list goes on and one--illustrates in the most dramatic form that none of us--civilians, diplomats, peacemakers alike--is immune from the scourge of international terrorism. Increasingly it seems to make little difference that the victims are unrelated in any real sense to the ultimate objectives of the terrorists. Increasingly terrorism is viewed as an appropriate instrument of state policy. The dangers posed by these awful phenomena underline the importance in seeking a better understanding of the terrorist threat so that we can cope with it more effectively.

One of the reasons why countering terrorism has proven so difficult is that we have allowed the proponents of terrorism to achieve what may be called "semantic infiltration." Understanding that they cannot grow and win support by parading their own values, terrorist movements and their supporters at the U.N., as elsewhere, concentrate on blurring issues and on systematically concealing their true identity and purposes. They sow confusion until, like a Trojan horse, they are able to penetrate our defenses. Subversion of language, our only means for rational thought, is their technique. Perhaps nowhere is this more painfully evident than at the United Nations, where we can observe directly how this process of subversion of language is honed to a fine art.

In this way, governments that are autocratic are called "democratic," policies intended to incite to war are deemed "peaceful," and that which is imposed by terror is termed "popular" and "progressive." Movements that are neither peaceful, popular, nor democratic are associated with words like "lasting peace" and "peoples' democracy." Extremists and terrorists, whose acts flout the letter and spirit of the U.N. Charter, find justification in U.N. resolutions which endorse the "use of all the necessary means at their disposal" to achieve so-called "self-determination" and "national liberation." Of course, this liberal disposition toward "all the necessary means" is selectively applied to those groups favored by the current U.N. majority.

Thus, in confronting the challenge of international terrorism the first step is to call things by their proper names and to see clearly and say plainly who the terrorists are, what goals they seek, and which governments support them. It is toward this end that I should like to address four widely-held misconceptions about terrorism.

The first misconception about terrorism involves the meaning of the world. It is said by a number of distinguished students of the subject that a rigorous and objective definition of terrorism is impossible. This is so, it is argued, because, "One man's terrorist is another man's freedom fighter." If we follow this line of logic, consensus about what is and is not terrorism becomes impossible and we are left suspended in a kind of intellectual and moral limbo. Terrorists want to push us into just such a limbo, because if no objective definition of terrorism exists, if we cannot even articulate what we mean by terrorism, then we cannot hope to stop it.

I believe that terrorism can be defined. It is true that efforts at consensus on defining international terrorism have not met with success, largely because of the attempt by "national liberation movements" to exclude violence from its definition. Nevertheless prominent Western thinkers have generally agreed on its distinguishing characteristics. For example, the International Law Association's Committee on International Terrorism would define an international terrorist act as one directed against any foreign government or international organization or any representative thereof, or against any national of a foreign country, simply because he is a national of a foreign country. The act involves murder, maiming, or menacing in order to gain political ends. Whether the act occurs in peacetime or wartime is immaterial, as is the political motivation of the actor. An even broader definition would seem appropriate. Terrorism should, I believe, be defined simply as the use or threatened use of violence for political purposes to extort, intimidate or coerce others in modifying their behavior. Under this definition terrorism starts at the lower end with the use or the threat of violence to acquire resources to pursue political objectives. It thus extends to the crimes of extortion and robbery, where the aim is political. The range includes hostage-taking, assassination, bombing, and threats by groups or individuals; and the indiscriminate use of violence against civilians by insurgent groups and paramilitary or military organizations. It extends at the top of the range to the terrorist acts of states, using instruments of state or non-state groups to promote national objectives.

Unfortunately, there is no real likelihood of achieving international agreement on this or any definition of terrorism. Various states in the Non-Aligned Movement (NAM) have sought to exclude groups engaged in "wars of national liberation" from the definition of terrorism.

Greece recently tried to get NATO agreement to a definition of terrorism that would distinguish between people or groups attempting to overthrow rightist regimes from those trying to overthrow leftist regimes. Both the Soviet Union and the People's Republic of China have refused in various international forums to relinquish their support of wars of national liberation. These states, and others, have prevented and can be expected to continue to prevent agreement on the definition of terrorism because they refuse to relinquish support for terrorist activity in selected political contexts--mostly in support of "wars of national liberation." This lack of a popular definition, this tendency to say "one man's terrorist is another man's freedom fighter," should not, however, deter us from our determination to define international terrorism as crimes against humanity regardless of motivation or political context.

A second misconception about terrorism is the widespread tendency to regard terrorists as "frustrated idealists," "desperate men" who turned to terrorism as an instrument of social progress only because they regretfully concluded that "the system doesn't work." Proponents of this point of view, while disassociating themselves from terrorist methods, are nevertheless quite willing to praise the courage, sincerity, and idealism of the terrorists themselves--provided, that is, that the terrorists openly identify with the radical left.

What advocates of the "frustrated idealist" school of thought fail to understand, however, is that terrorists are not at all interested in social progress. They have a different goal. They want to destroy existing political institutions, especially when they are democratic. The Red Brigades, after all, killed Aldo Moro, a center-liberal political, and not some monarchist fanatic. In truth, the aim of most terrorists is not to hasten progress, but to provoke a repressive or fascist reaction. The goal of the Baader-Meinhof groups was not German reform but rebirth from the ashes. For the Palestinian terrorists, the goal is not a more benevolent Israeli policy or a Palestinian Arab state coexisting with a Jewish state and with Jordan, it is

the elimination of Israel.   For the violent Irish Republican
Army militant, the aim is not civil rights for Catholics in
Northern Ireland, but the end of Northern Ireland as a
separate political entity.

    A third misconception about terrorism is the notion
that terrorist actions arise from troubled social conditions.
To be sure, terrorists exploit adverse economic and social
conditions to their advantage.   But terrorist outrages are
principally aimed at American, British, Dutch, German,
Italian, Spanish, and Israeli nationals.   None of these
societies is perfect, but they are the least imperfect--and
among the most enlightened, progressive, and democratic--
in the world.   The worst societies in the world tend to be
the freest from terrorism.   As the former Soviet freedom
fighter, Valdimir Bukovsky, has observed, "Where there are
real tyrants, and the worst oppression, we do not see such
violence."   Terrorist violence is aimed almost exclusively
at democratic or pro-Western regimes, while Communist and
pro-Soviet regimes are left almost entirely unscathed.
Moreover, the level of training and organization that has
enabled international terrorism to challenge established
governments is simply beyond the ability of local, isolated
terrorist groups.   International terrorism is inconceivable
apart from the financial support, military training, and
sanctuary provided to the terrorists by certain states.   To
seek the causes of terrorism in the behavior of societies
victimized by terrorism is thus to look in the wrong place.
Rather, these causes are to be found in the convictions and
expectations of the terrorists themselves, and in the
activities of those states that find it in their interest to
support international terrorism--that is, the Soviet Union,
its Eastern European allies, and other states such as Libya,
Syria, Iran, Iraq, North Korea, the People's Democratic
Republic of Yemen, Cuba, and Nicaragua.

    To these sources of confusion must be added yet
another misconception--the notion that democratic societies can easily cope with the challenge of terrorism.   We
sometimes hear that there is nothing to worry about.
Terrorism, it is argued, is a marginal, largely irrelevant
phenomenon with little or no impact on the democratic

political process. This complacent attitude toward terrorism--this belief that modern, democratic, industrial societies can easily cope with a handful of terrorist malcontents--is profoundly mistaken. West Germany's former Chancellor, Helmut Schmidt, was nearer the mark when he observed in 1976 that the revolutionary left posed the greatest challenge to German democracy since its creation.   Chancellor Schmidt understood that a systematic campaign of terrorism can undermine the moral consensus that underlies any democratic political order, that popular irritation and fear generated by disorder and chaos could well provoke a reaction by those who believe that democracy is unable to defend itself or society.   In several European and Latin American states small numbers of revolutionaries, disdainful of the electoral process and unable to win popular support through the ballot box in any case, have succeeded in converting the climate of opinion from one that sustains parliamentary debate into one that encourages blows and counterblows, violence and counter-violence, and a resultant breakdown in parliamentary institutions.

Clearly, the Soviet Union and its allies all have grasped the potential of terrorist movements for disrupting societies, particularly in the so-called Third World. Clearly, they have recognized that throughout Asia, Africa, and Latin America, there are weak governments with low levels of legitimacy and high levels of instability. To a degree far greater than is generally realized, these governments are actuely vulnerable to terrorist disruptions, and are therefore inviting targets to terrorist campaigns. In providing terrorist movements with arms, training, and political support, the Soviet Union and its allies have thus discovered a highly "cost-effective" way of making the point that in today's world it is not safe to practice democracy.   In this regard it is of interest to note that in a list of 10 nations prepared by the U.S. Department of State as supporting terrorist groups or using terrorism as an instrument of state policy, only Iran is not directly or closely associated with the Soviet Union.   And among all of these states there appears to be an increasing common turn to not only providing sanctuary to terrorists but to directly using terrorism as an instrument of national policy.

While no "smoking gun" is ever likely to be presented as proof, the evidence is strong that Syria and Iran supported or encouraged the bombing of Multi-National Force units in Beirut. The North Koreans got caught in Rangoon--caught with two of their army officers at the site of a bombing attempt on the President and high officials of South Korea. There are indications of possible Iranian involvement in the bombings in Kuwait which included a truck-bomb attack on the American Embassy and six other bomb attacks at the same time, mainly against Kuwaiti targets. There are also indications of Syrian support for the Black June Group. To be sure, the great majority of incidents is still by terrorist groups acting on their own, but state-sponsored terrorism has been responsible for the greatest number of assassinations and murders in recent years. The resort to extreme violence in terrorism appears to be directed or controlled and undertaken by states or groups which are significantly supported by states.

What measures, then, can be taken on the international front, in multilateral forums and especially at the U.N., to protect the potential victims of international terrorism? As I have intimated, at the United Nations we can expect only limited progress at best. This is not to say that significant advances have not been made. In December 1979 a significant victory was scored when the United Nations adopted the International Convention Against the Taking of Hostages. The basic thrust of the Hostage Convention is that those who take hostages will be subject to prosecution or extradition if they are apprehended within the jurisdiction of a state party to the Convention, regardless of the motives of the hijacker. But beyond the Hostage Convention, and the 1973 U.N. Convention on the Prevention and Punishment of Crimes Against Internationally Protected Persons, including Diplomatic Agents, little progress has been made. Attempts to reach consensus on an internationally acceptable definition of terrorism has continually been stymied by those who seek exceptions for so-called "political offenders."

The difficulty the United States delegation to the United Nations encountered in the 1981 General Assembly session when a resolution was introduced regarding the U.S. Government's decision to extradite a Palestinian fugitive, Ziad Abu Eain, to stand trial in Israel for alleged acts of terrorism illustrates the reluctance of the U.N. to act. Mr. Abu Eain had been indicted by an Israeli court for murder on the grounds of having allegedly planted a bomb in Tiberias, Israel, which killed two youths and injured more than 30 others. After an exhaustive judicial procedure in the U.S., whereby three different courts held that sufficient evidence existed to warrant the indictment, Mr. Abu Eain was ordered to be extradicted. Nevertheless, despite strong U.S. opposition, the U.N. General Assembly, on December 15, 1981, adopted by a vote of 75-21 (with 43 abstentions) a resolution which "strongly deplored the action of the Government of the United States." In addition, it "reaffirmed the legitimacy of the struggle for independence, territorial integrity, national unity, and liberation from colonial and foreign domination and alien subjugation by all available means."

Multilateral efforts at securing an internationally acceptable definition of terrorism cannot succeed as long as states cling to exceptions for "national liberation movements" and other politically inspired actions. Rather, we should devote our efforts to strengthening regional conventions and bilateral agreements. Even in regional forums, where the more radical voices heard at the U.N. are not present, there continues to be a tendency to accept the notion that the political nature of a terrorist act can excuse the crime. Thus the 1978 European Convention on Suppression of Terrorism permits signatory parties to make reservations based on the political offense exception. It is essential that we be clear about who the terrorists are, what goals they seek, and which governments support them. Much has already been done in separating myth from fact, claim from reality, lie from truth about terrorists and their goals. Pioneering work has been done on the aspect of state-supported terrorism. In their recently published book, *Terrorism as State Sponsored Covert Warfare*, Ray

Cline and Yonah Alexander ably document what the title suggests. We can do more. More attention needs to be called to state-supported terrorism. States practicing such behavior must be made to understand that it is unacceptable.

By working together, we who see the free individual and the free society as our purpose and guiding principle should be able to render the intimidators and practitioners of terror less capable of harm, and establish the dream of a society of free states and free men and women more secure.

PART THREE
JEWISH PERSPECTIVE

CHAPTER V

The Hagana and the War for Israel's Independence

N. Lorch

About fourteen years ago, I was at the United Nations as Israel's representative in the Third Committee. There was a debate about terrorism, and I gave my report. The Syrian ambassador got up and holding a copy of my book about the war of independence said, "This ambassador, he is not an ambassador, he is a colonel, he is a terrorist." I thanked him politely for promoting my book and continued. I don't think the Hagana has to defend itself for having been a terrorist organization. The Hagana was an organization which was in existence for 28 years. It started in 1920 when the Hashomer, a small, elitist, and closed group, dissolved and the Hagana came into being as a mass movement. The Hagana ceased to exist in 1948 when it was converted into the Israeli army. The twenty-eight years of the Hagana's existence was a time of immense change in the World and in Israel, and the Hagana changed with the times. From its start when the population of Jews in Palestine was barely 100,000 people to 1948 at its end when it numbered over 650,000 members, the Hagana was continually changing and growing. The Hagana started with a few pistols and some stocks and stones and ended with an underground air force, an underground navy, and artillery.

The Hagana was an illegal underground movement from the very beginning and it was never in compliance with British policy. However, the Hagana was not designed to operate contrary to British wishes or fight against the British except for a short significant period between issuance of the White Paper of 1939 and the outbreak of World War II, and later from the end of World War II until 1947. During most of its existence, the Hagana was designed to defend the Jewish population of Palestine against Arab attacks.

To the extent the British compiled with their obligations under the mandate to preserve law and order in the country and to protect Jewish lives and property, the Hagana became quiescient and, at times, even cooperative. To the extent the British diverged from their commitments, or their commitments as we saw them, the relations with the British became more and more tense, and of course, proportionately the underground became much deeper. The objectives changed, from defending existing values into the defense of rights of aspirations. The Hagana undertook to defend the rights of the Jewish people to immigrate into Palestine, not just to defend those who were already there. Subsequently the Hagana undertook to arm and train Jews to enable them to defend themselves. At one time the Hagana cooperated with the British in the fight against the Axis powers. The Hagana recruited parachutists for operations with the British against Germany behind enemy lines in Europe. At one time the Hagana even undertook to plan and prepare for the defense of Palestine against the possibility of a Nazi attack. There was no need to implement that plan, but in the files of the Hagana, one will find documents showing how the Hagana thought it could defend the Jewish population of Palestine in case of a British withdrawal in 1941. In other words, the objectives changed, the doctrine changed, the arsenal changed, the composition changed. Constant was the fact that we were an illegal underground. There was never any thought that the decision in our struggle with the British would be brought about by arms alone. There was an ongoing political debate and the idea was basically to convince

public opinion in Great Britain and elsewhere that the
policy of the British government was wrong.   Therefore, as
far as the British were concerned, not only was the policy of
the Hagana to minimize British casualties, but civilian
casualties were totally forbidden.

Consider the Night of the Bridges, when the Jewish
Resistance Movement undertook to blow up all the bridges
leading from Palestine into neighboring countries, the idea
was not to cause any British casualties; the idea was to
prove to the British and to the world that here was a well-
organized and determined organization, and they would be
well-advised to change their policy, otherwise there would
be a bloody war on their hands.   Another example is the
passive resistance of illegal immigrants.   The Hagana
undertook to bring illegal immigrant ships to Palestine, and
when they were caught and boarded by British personnel,
the instructions were "Do not oppose the British by force."
Passive resistance, yes, but no British casualties.   Because
basically this was an argument in a political debate.   These
fluctuations in the relations with the British sometimes
went to paradoxical lengths.   There was a time during the
Second World War when the Hagana cooperated with one
part of the British establishment to fight against the Nazis,
on   the   condition   that   another   part   of   the   British
establishment, namely the colonial government, would not
know the details.   When the Palmach was established in
1941 with British help, the condition was that those British
officers who cooperated in the training of the Palmach in
preparation for war against the Germans, would not inform
the colonial government of the names of those who were in
the Palmach because they might have been arrested and
tried.   It might be said, the British intelligence officers
who worked with us did not reveal to their British
colleagues those things they were not supposed to.   This
was not typical by any means, after El Alamein when the
danger of German invasion of Palestine receded, the special
relationship with certain branches of the British military
establishment cooled considerably.   This is but one illustration of the complexities of the relationship with the
mandatory government at that time.

Another important point is that the Hagana, from the outset, considered itself as a mass movement. In the fundamental principles, the "Oshyot" of the Hagana, which every one of us was supposed to learn by heart, says that it is "the right and the duty of every man and woman in Israel" (the word Israel here is interesting, because we're not referring to the land or the country, the state of Israel which was not yet in existence, but it was left open whether the Jews in the Diaspora had the game right and duty) "to be a member of the Hagana."   This of course, was a very complicated undertaking; you want an underground which has to be maintained as a secret and, on the other hand, it is the right and duty of everybody to join.   Acceptance was on an individual basis, it was not automatic, and there were stratifications of secrecy.   We were trained to use arms illegally, but we were not supposed to know where those arms were to be hidden, once we had finished using them. This was supposedly a strict secret as far as we were concerned, because in this mass movement, there were circles and concentric circles of secrecy, and in order to try and maintain some sort of a possible defense against leaks. Again, this fluctuated; there were times that the British were actively engaged in the persecution of the Hagana, there were times when they knew and didn't care very much. All of us who were members of the Hagana would remember the coded messages as, "your aunt invites you to a birthday party at 6 a.m. tomorrow morning, please provide broom and cherries."   Now, anybody who's ever attended an aunt's birthday party, would probably know what that means.   The Hagana considered itself the only unified military organization of the Yishuv and Zionist movement.   This is where the major debate, which sometimes became more than a debate, with the Irgun and the Lechi arose.   The Hagana considered itself the only unified organization entitled to be the military arm of the Yishuv.   The Hagana tried to maintain democratic control of its underground organization and this was a very complex undertaking considering how complicated it is to control any military organization by a democratic body in a modern state.   It is far more complicated to do so in the case of an underground, where the political leadership is openly elected, known to everybody, and where the military leadership and the membership must be totally unknown and anonymous. However, the Hagana consistently tried but it did not always succeed in maintaining democratic control of a democratically-elected body over the operations of the organization. At first, the political body was a party, called the Labor Party, then it was the Labor Federation, then from the end of the '20s onward, it was the "Vaada Paritetit"--the 50/50 Committee, which was made up 50% of the representatives of the Labor Parties in Palestine, and 50% of the civilian parties of the country. At the time of the Resistance movement, which was the joint movement of the three organizations (Hagana, Irgun, and Lechi) operations were controlled by a Committee whose composition was unknown but which had been appointed by the properly-elected authorities of the country. This is probably a unique phenomenon, that an underground organization maintained its being subject to the direction of a democratically-elected body. The Hagana, to the best of its ability, practiced what was called the Sanctity of Arms, which basically had two major elements; one was the preservation of arms. Arms were very difficult to obtain, and arms had to be preserved, to be guarded, to be cleaned, and under no circumstances given away.

The other element was the purity of arms, namely that arms should not be used except when it was absolutely necessary. In relations with the Arabs, the concrete content of "purity of arms" varied according to circumstance; there was no one single, static doctrine. At the beginning it signified static defense, that is, the defense of every settlement must be conducted on its perimeter. It changed to going "beyond the fence," that is, not waiting inside until you're attacked, but erecting an ambush or preemptive attack against somebody who wants to attack you. Then it escalated to "retaliation against the guilty." When Arabs besieged Jerusalem, we besieged Jaffa, and in the end, there were operations to capture territory which was allocated to the Jewish state and hold it. In other words, the concrete content of purity of arms changed in accordance with circumstances, but the principle of purity of arms was maintained throughout.

What is interesting is the fact that the purity of arms was never regarded as a purely or merely moral principle. There was a constant search to find pragmatic justifications for certain principles, for the principle of purity of arms.   I will enumerate some of these considerations which were used as arguments or justifications for the purity of arms. One was education; there were leaders in the Hagana who said we must not spoil the youth which is entrusted to us and, therefore, they must never be told to use arms in vain, only if it is absolutely necessary. Another one was on political grounds; if we used arms indeliberately, it would strengthen those elements within the British administration who were looking for an excuse to come down on the Jews of Palestine.   Another one is a matter of public relations; we needed international support, we wanted political support and sympathetic public opinion throughout the world. Another one is that to the extent we used violence against Arabs who have not been actively involved in the fight against us, we would help Arab activist leaders and Arab terrorists to gain support amongst their own population. Therefore, in order to isolate Arab activists, we had to refrain from indiscriminate use of violence.   And, last but not least, I don't know whether this was entirely serious, but Ben Gurion, at one point, said whoever uses violence wantonly against Arabs will ultimately use violence wantonly against Jews.   In other words, the purity of arms was a moral principle, but there was a deliberate attempt to justify it on pragmatic utilitarian grounds.

These principles were constant elements in the history of the Hagana.   It was an underground, it was illegal, it operated contrary to British policies, it avoided throughout most of its existence operating against the British.   Where it operated against the British, it was primarily as an argument in a debate and, therefore, it was strictly limited to certain objectives which would gain or help gain support, if not in Great Britain, at least in other countries and, above all, in the United States.   The Hagana was designed from the outset as a mass movement; it had specialized units for special purposes. But the organization as such was designed as a mass movement, even when there were only a couple of hundred members. The concept was one of an organization for the defense of the entire Yishuv. It considered itself as the unified military arm of the Yishuv and World Zionist Movement. It was under democratic control. It tried, to the best of its ability, to preserve the sanctity of arms, including the purity of arms. I do not claim that this was strictly applied in practice; in such a mass organization there were cases in which this was not observed. But, by and large, there was an aspiration to do that and when there were divergences or infractions, they were dealt with firmly. I will end with a quote from Natah Alterman, who said, "Just because war is cruel, the principles of mercy, and honesty, must be applied with equal cruelty."

CHAPTER VI

The IZL and Its Role in the Liberation of Israel form the British Rule

Professor J. Nedava

To do justice to the Irgun Zevai L'eumi (IZL), the National Military Organization, in evaluating its share in the establishment of the State of Israel, one has to dwell at some length on its aims, its antecedents, and the vicissitudes it experienced during the years of its existence. All this has been inextricably interwoven with the history of Zionism for a number of years. Without reviewing its background, one can hardly conceive the raison d'etre of the IZL.

One can conveniently divide the years of the IZL's activity into three distinct periods. The first one extended over the period 1931-1937, under the command of Abraham T'homi. The second period covered the years 1938-1940, under the command of David Raziel. The last and most crucial period of the IZL extended over the years 1944-1948, under the command of Menachem Begin, until the IZL's dismantlement and the incorporation of its battalions into Israel's Defense Force.

A most intriguing problem is the attempt to draw a demarcation line between a terrorist organization and a genuine movement of national liberation, and another problem closely related--concerns a morality test to be applied to differentiate the nature and types of such organizations. These problems may seem insoluble, for the nature of terroristic acts and their possible legitimacy are variously defined by philosophers, scholars, and politicians, and we are dealing with values projected on a relative scale.

The IZL was an organization of national liberation par excellence. Its aims were fundamentally political. Mr. Begin, too, was first and foremost a political activist. The IZL was established in order to serve as an instrument for the liberation of the Land of Israel from its foreign occupier. Today, the designation "foreign occupier" has become part and parcel of a universally accepted nomenclature in the context of Zionism's evolvement over the years, but it was certainly a revolutionary concept when it was first broached immediately following the Arab riots in 1929. 1929 was a watershed in the history of the British-Zionist relationship. Until that year most of the Zionist leaders were still basking in the euphoria of a political "honeymoon," faithfully believing that Britain would ultimately fulfill pledges undertaken in the Balfour Declaration of 1917, and the Mandate of 1922. It was generally assumed that despite disappointments and frustrations, the inherent identity of interests of both Zionism and the British Empire remained unimpaired. In 1929, it first dawned on a few of the Zionist thinkers that the apparently idyllic relationship was a mere illusion. Following the 1929 riots, those endowed with foresight aired for the first time what seemed a bizarre and disharmonious view, namely, that the breach between Britain and Zionism was real. One could no longer trust Britain to discharge its obligations. Consequently, Zionism stood no chance of getting support for the implementation of the "Jewish National Home" unless its leaders embarked on a new path, the unavoidable path of revolt and armed resistance. It was then that the term "foreign or alien occupier" was first coined. This new concept also necessitated a change in the course of action: the target was no longer the local Arab population, but rather the British Palestine Administration.

One has to be reminded that Britain was not legally the sovereign ruler of Palestine, but its Mandatory Power, acting in the capacity of a trustee on behalf of the League of Nations, Palestine never constituted a part of the British Empire. British rule there was conditioned by its fulfillment of the basic undertaking to establish in Palestine, over both sides of the Jordan River, the "Jewish National Home" (which originally connoted a Jewish State, as was amply confirmed in later years by several authoritative British statesmen). The final irreparable breach between Britain and Zionism occurred in 1939 with the publication of the White Paper of that year. Under its terms Britain had reneged on its solemn pledges to the Jewish people. Not only was the promise to convert Palestine into a Jewish state disregarded, but, more explicitly, it was announced that "the objective of His Majesty's Government is the establishment within 10 years of an independent Palestine (i.e., an Arab) state." A final group of 75,000 Jews would be admitted into the country, but all further Jewish immigration would come to end "unless the Arabs of Palestine are prepared to acquiesce in it." Similarly, an almost absolute ban on the purchase of lands by Jews would come into effect. Thus, the IZL, not having any political alternative, now set on resorting to violent means with the object of forcing Britain either to change its policy radically, or else face the threat of being driven out of Palestine as a "foreign occupier."

Emphasis should also be put on the high moral standards that the IZL set for itself from the very beginning of its revolt. This marks the all-important difference between the IZL and a terrorist organization such as the PLO, which does not admit any inhibitions in the use of force. We must recall the highly-motivated principles that Jabotinsky bequeathed his disciples. He considered himself a liberal of the 19th century brand, whose main tenet consisted in fostering sanctity of human life. In his youth he counted himself as a protagonist of the anarchistic persuasion and pacifism. He always preached the need to carry on the struggle for human rights in the open, believing that all governments can be persuaded to change their course through the exertion of political pressure. Viewing the public arena from such an angle, he was naturally opposed to all undergrounds, not excluding any operating within the Zionist fold.   At best the creation of the Hagana, and later of the IZL, were considered by him as a kind of a lesser evil, expedient only under the circumstances that no other way was open to ward off Arab attacks against the Yishuv (the Jewish population in Palestine).   Jabotinsky also opposed the policy of indiscriminate retaliation against the local Arab population aimed at the avenging of the murder of Jews.   A plan was once submitted to him for confirmation, directed at Haj Amin El-Husseini, the Mufti of Jerusalem, arch enemy of Zionism and the hand behind the brutal murders of Jews.   Jabotinsky refused to sanction the assassination.   In 1938, following the British execution of a youngster--Shelomo Ben-Yosef, the first Jewish martyr under the Mandatory--Jabotinsky changed his mind and agreed reluctantly to the commission of acts of retaliation by the IZL.

Mr. Begin adopted a similar moral approach to events throughout the years he headed the IZL.   In his proclamation of the revolt on February 1, 1944, he stressed IZL's determination to spare civilian lives, including those of British officialdom, at all costs.   Time and again he vouched for a "clean" fight.   IZL's first actions were directed against Government buildings (Immigration, Income Tax, and Police Offices) and as a rule, prior notice of the forthcoming action was given to all concerned to alert the occupants in time to leave the premises.   If Mr. Begin was willing to delude himself that a military struggle for national liberation against a foreign occupier could be carried out without casualties, he was soon robbed of his illusion.   The first IZL casualty occurred during an attack of the CID building in Jerusalem; and it soon became evident that pious and sanctimonious declarations about the sanctity of human life were of no avail in the face of sombre reality, and that acts of violence were by their very nature epidemic.   The blowing up by IZL of a whole wing of the King David Hotel in Jerusalem exacted a cruel toll of life-- over 90 casualties.

In 1947 Mr. Begin was in a predicament, faced with a sensitive moral issue, when required to decide the fate of

two British hostages held by the IZL.   Despite his natural
tendency to relent, he encountered the situation coura-
geously.   He felt that the entire fate of the IZL hung in the
balance, and that retreat on his part would affect the
organization's credibility.   I remember discussing Mr.
Begin's dilemma with Arthur Koestler at his London home.
You may recall that the author of *Darkness at Noon* was a
protagonist of IZL and at the same time a moralist, whose
major works are much concerned with ethical issues.
Koestler was convinced that in the wake of the execution of
the three condemned IZL members, Mr. Begin had no choice
but to reply in kind.   Had he acted differently, it was
doubtful that the IZL could survive.   The IZL fanatical
tenacity proved that it was intent on fighting to the bitter
end, come what may.   In retrospect, the hanging of the two
British sergeants on August 1, 1947, represented a breaking
point of the entire struggle.   In *Britain's Moment in the
Middle East*, Elizabeth Monroe wrote: "The British public
had taken Palestine in its stride for years....   But on August
1, 1947, its attitude changed, and the cause of the change
was the hanging of two young sergeants whom Jewish
terrorists executed as a reprisal ... by September it
[Britain] had changed its mind and announced that it was
giving up the Mandate."

A few years ago I published a paper dealing with a
highly controversial subject relating to recent Zionist
history.   I was trying to determine the share of each of the
three Jewish underground movements in the Yishuv's effort
to bring about the relinquishment of the Palestine Mandate.
In the wake of the recent opening of the confidential British
official state archives, the issue in question can amply be
resolved.   But I intentionally refrained from drawing on
those confidential papers, for I was sure that even the open
records were sufficient for our purpose.   In order to make
things even simpler, I limited myself to gauging British
public opinion over the critical period of July 22, 1946 (the
day of the King David blow-up) to August 1, 1947.   I make,
however, haste to point out that the official documents
recently made public generally tend to substantiate my
thesis: the IZL served as a catalyst, precipitating British

evacuation from Palestine by 10 years, and, by the same token, expediting Israel's rise to independence by that extent. At the end of 1947 and beginning of 1948 I paid extensive visits to London where I had an opportunity to watch the British scene at close quarters. At the end of World War II in 1945, Britain was losing ground and beating a retreat from most of its former highly-regarded strategic positions. The Empire was emerging from a gigantic struggle weakened almost to the point of exhaustion. The British economy was in shambles, characterized by a cold, fuelless winter, causing public suffering from some basic shortages. It soon transpired that the Labour Government would be forced to embark on a policy of retrenchment. This, naturally, indirectly played into the hands of the IZL.

At this context it is worth noting that the IZL was very fortunate from the very beginning in facing the British as antagonists. The situation might have been totally different had the occupier been France, Germany, Belgium, let alone a totalitarian power such as the Soviet Union. By virtue of its inbred liberal tradition, Britain was ill-disposed to fight what Churchill called "squalid warfare with terrorists." He wrote, "No country in the world is less fit for a conflict with terrorists than Great Britain. That is not because of her weakness or cowardice; it is because of her restraint and the way of life which we have lived so long in this shattered island." It was therefore a foregone conclusion that Britain would sooner or later relinquish what seemed to be to all intents and purposes a useless post. The popular press in Britain, and a great number of MPs on both sides of the aisle, persistently called for an early British withdrawal from Palestine. Here are a few examples: Kenneth Lindsay--"I had the definite feeling that the time had come when my countrymen ought not to stay in that country and be shot at." Sir Thomas Moore-- "Why do we continue to expose our soldiers and civilians to savage murder in Palestine for no apparent return except hatred from the Jews?" Sir Waldron Smithers--"May I ask the right hon. gentleman whether His Majesty's Government will ... admit their failure by clearing out?" Oliver Stanley--"I would prefer that we should clear out of

Palestine and tell the people of the world that we are unable to carry out our Mandate there." Churchill spoke of the burden being "too heavy for one single country to bear," and then, on another occasion, "How long does the Secretary of State for the Colonies expect that this state of squalid warfare with all its bloodshed will go on, at a cost of L30 million or L40 million a year, keeping 100,000 Englishmen away with the military forces?"

The effect of the IZL's and LEHI's staggering activity from day to day was devastating. In his report from Palestine, following the storming of the Acre prison in May 1947, the *New York Times* correspondent Clifton Daniel compared the Jewish heroic feat with the historic fall of the French Bastille in 1789. There were, of course, some other opinions which were voiced in Britain and elsewhere with the object of helping to salvage the country from its dire predicament, but these were on the whole, faint cries in the wilderness. For instance, such a prestigious military authority as Field-Marshal Montgomery, the hero of El-Amein, proposed an all-out onslaught against the three Jewish undergrounds in Palestine with a view to stamping out terrorism, even at the risk of ruining the entire Yishuv; but he, too, felt "that if we were not prepared to maintain law and order in Palestine, it would be better to get out," and that was also the determined stand of the Palestine High Commissioner, General Sir Alan Cunnningham.

In my paper I was further trying to establish a comparative scale of intensity, measuring the repercussions which had been stirred by IZL and LEHI on the one hand, and the Hagana, whose struggle against the British hinged mainly on the front of the so-called Jewish illegal immigration into Palestine, on the other. My rough estimate was--though not based on actual statistics--that some 90 percent of all press coverage and parliamentary proceedings during the testing period (July 22, 1946 to August 1, 1947) dealt with what was called "terrorism" proper, as compared with 10 percent coverage dealing with cases of so-called illegal immigration. Of course, the Exodus affair made a tremendous impact on world opinion and it engaged world attention for many days. I by no means intend to minimize the historic role played by the Hagana--its constructive work over a long period of time, the influence and strength it exerted on behalf of Israel's independence, its accumulation of arms, its conduct of critical military training, and all of the other preparations for the ultimate showdown with the Arabs, both in Palestine and the surrounding countries, in order to safeguard Israel's nascent independence in days to come. Here we are discussing the pre-Israeli period, however, trying to appraise the developments which brought about the evacuation of Britain from Palestine, and, as stated above, it is my considered opinion that IZL hastened the withdrawal by 10 years. I leave it to you to speculate as to what might have happened, had IZL and LEHI not been privileged to play that role. History records the sequence of events that actually take place, and rarely indulges in imaginative speculations about the "ifs" and the "might have beens."

CHAPTER VII

Lechi's Share in the Struggle for Israel's Liberation

Dr. Z. Iviansky

The underground, the FFI (in Hebrew, Lechi) has been relatively shortlived, and its history was probably the most tragic of all modern movements. An essay entitled 'What was Lechi, and who was Yair?' published in *Sulam* (February 1962), written by Professor Israel Eldad, one of Lechi's top leaders, states: "Lechi and its struggle lasted seven years. Lechi was the smallest of all Israeli underground movements, but the most influential in thought and deed. It's decline and demise was shocking and painful. It disintegrated," writes Eldad, in a style reminiscent of one of Yair's poems, "on the torn remnants of a purple carpet, among the leaves of a trampled lily."[1]

Painful as it certainly must have been to many of its members, Lechi vanished, and died a natural death as soon as it had completed its task and fulfilled its destiny. Its struggle lasted seven years from the time of its establishment, when it was born out of a split in the NMO 'Irgun' in June 1940. It knew times of failure, tragic entanglements, the death and imprisonment of the core of its leadership, the desertion of many others, and--the final blow--the tragic end of its leader Avraham Stern (Yair), murdered while handcuffed and disarmed, by the British police.   Then came its revival at the end of 1942, through continuing strife and struggles, through ebbs and flows, successes, climaxes, and painful losses and defeats, until its final disintegration with the establishment of the State of Israel.

Today, its former leaders are dispersed among almost all the shades and colors of the political spectrum from left to right, while one of its leaders, the man who organized and molded the crushed remnants into a powerful underground organization again, became the Prime Minister of the Government of Israel. In a talk given at the 'Conference of the Fighters,' held in April 1949, Yitzhak Shamir refers to the impossible task which he faced when he made his first escape from prison in 1942: "I have recently read Begin's reminiscences in which he relates how they started with 400 men, several machine guns, some tons of explosives and a hundred guns," says Shamir. "What did we have to start with? 400? That would have been a dream for us. We didn't even have 40! Did we possess even one machine gun? Did we even have 10 kilograms of explosives?!"[2]

This, then, was the state of affairs towards the close of 1942. We also have Shamir's testimony of the state of affairs a year earlier, towards the end of 1941, a few days before Shamir was himself caught and arrested. In an interview in *Ma'ariv* of February 3, 1967, marking the 25th anniversary of Yair's death, Shamir relates how he met Yair on a dark, cloudy night during a wartime blackout, and how they strolled along the city streets which were their usual meeting places. "Yair," said Shamir, "was talking with complete certainty of his imminent death. I shall never forget his words. 'When they catch me they are going to kill me straight away and present the excuse that I tried to escape....' He was absolutely calm. I can remember every word of his. He said: 'Never mind! Our example will inspire many others to continue the struggle. I am absolutely confident that the struggle will not come to an end with my death, but will rather gain power....' He even explained something we were able to understand only after his death: 'Struggle does not dissipate strength: it engenders it.'"[3]

Avraham Stern (Yair) the venerated ideologist, politician, leader of the NMO (Irgun), then of Lechi, knew clearly and with certainty what lay ahead. He was aware of his fate many years before he encountered it because he had chosen it. Stern was a poet. In *Anonymous Soldiers*, written in 1932, one of his first poems, later to become the anthem of the NMO, then of Lechi--almost all the elements of his future life and fate are revealed. The refrain runs, in a word-for-word translation, as follows:

> In the red days of the pogrom-riots and blood,
> In the dark nights of despair
> We shall raise our flag in villages and in towns,
> Inscribing, there; Defense and Conquest.[4]

The red days were of the slaughter and of the massacre of our people; the dark nights were those of the terrible despair that has been the well-spring of our struggles and our wars; of the continuous, tragic, and desperate ordeal in defense of existence.

Lechi arose in one of those darkest hours. Describing those times, the historian of the Hagana opens the chapter about the "post-White Paper" period: "In the few months preceding the outbreak of the Second World War, the Zionist movement and the Jewish community in Israel found themselves in a deep political crisis. Negotiations which had been continuing with the British Government failed and ended with the proclamation of the White Paper in May 1939. With this proclamation, 21 years of cooperation with Britain came to an end. The price of this breach of alliance" the historian continues, "was paid with the blood and soul of European Jewry, and resulted in the elimination of the source of our national strength and the cutting off of any hope for the future."[5] When I try to find a telling characterization of that tragic, desperate historical instance, I can find none better than that of Victor Serge,[6] the anarchist revolutionary, who conjures, "Living in a world without any possible escape, in which there was nothing left but to fight for an impossible escape." Here it is interesting to juxtapose the reply of Yehoshua Cohen--

one of Lechi's most renowned heroes, later a pioneer in the desert settlement of Sde Boker--when I questioned him about his past terrorist activities, and about the way in which they complemented his later activities as a settler-kibbutz pioneer, he said: "To be a pioneer means to adopt denigrated activities which seem impossible. This is what I have been doing throughout my life, in the past, and in Lechi, and at present also in Sde Boker."

Two outstanding personalities made almost identical statements at the time. They came from opposite political poles, and were for years bitter political opponents. Later they both became a Prime Minister of Israel: David Ben-Gurion and Menachem Begin. In September 1938, at the "Beitar" Conference in Warsaw, Begin contended the following: "The Jewish National Movement began with 'practical Zionism.' Then came 'political Zionism,' and now we stand at the threshold of 'military Zionism.'[7] Events will inevitably come to open confrontation ... otherwise Zionism will be eliminated." In April 1939, Ben-Gurion made a similar statement: "After the era of 'hibat-zion' (which means romantic, practical Zionism), and the subsequent era of 'political Zionism,' we are now at the threshold of a new era; the era of 'militant Zionism.'" A year later, at the conference of the Zionist Executive Committee, he made his statement more explicit: "There is now only one hope for Zionism--only if it becomes 'militant Zionism.' The Zionism of lofty ideas and empty phrases will not last."[8]

The question then was how to transform 'lofty Zionism' into 'fighting Zionism' against Britain, which at that crucial and most dangerous moment in the history of the Jewish people betrayed and abandoned it to its tragic fate. However, simultaneously, Britain was the only power left fighting Israel's bitterest enemy of all times--Nazi Germany. It was a tragic situation: Britain could continue to hunt Jewish refugees, expel them from the shores of their place of last hope, and still be certain that the Jews would continue to stand firmly at their side, because, as Malcolm MacDonald put it: "They had no choice." Lechi arose out of that historical trap. In his

illegal radio transmission of August 1941, Yair echoed Ben-
Gurion and Begin.   "The times of Mapai's 'hibat-zion,' and
the Revisionist's 'political Zionism,' are over.   It is now
the turn of 'fighting Zionism.'"   For him, however, that
meant that "the Hebrew Nation can be redeemed, and the
Hebrew State revived, only if the nation itself will dare to
begin fighting against the foes of Zionism."[9]   Yair felt that
there could be no unconditional alliance, and that an
unconditional alliance with Britain would bring about the
physical extermination of the Jewish people in Europe, and
the extinction of any hope for the future.   He stated
clearly, "As much as a change in British policy can induce us
to mobilize all our forces in her favor--so, too, the
continuation of her present policy can only bring about a
terrible catastrophe."[10]   Thus, there started a desperate
armed clash with all its tragic and inevitable results.

To compare and assess the choice made, I can find no
better example than that of the Russian revolutionary,
Andrei Zhelyabov (one of the leaders and victims of the
"People's Will" organization), who described their adoption
of terrorism as "the worst possible alternative in the most
impossible historical circumstances." In making his
choice, Yair knew with certainly that he was dooming his
personal fate and the fate of his closest friends. Was it a
suicidal decision? It was, as far as his own life was
concerned. "We know that our road will not be lined with
roses.... We know that we are going to face imprisonment
and the gallows....", he writes in one of the issues of Lechi's
clandestine journal, *In the Underground*, "But we shall not
retreat because we are definitely convinced of the justness
of our cause. We are certain of victory." Yet they also
felt that victory was to come "over their dead bodies," as
another Russian revolutionary, A. Mikhailov, had put it.   In
the *Underground*, No 5, of January 1941, the translation of a
few passages from P.S. O'Hegarty's book, *The Victory of
Sinn Fein* (Dublin, 1924) was published. Though the
passages dealt with the Irish Easter Rebellion of 1916, they
could be strongly related to the situation of Lechi in 1941.

"The Rebellion exploded upon the Irish people....
They did not expect it, neither did they want it....
If Ireland at that week of Rebellion could have
laid hands on Tom Clark and his associates, they
would have torn them to pieces....   The Rebellion
of 1916 had been, from its start, a lost cause, and a
voluntary sacrifice of their blood.   Those who
planned and led it did not hope for victory.   They
knew that they were not going to win.   They knew
that they might mount the scaffold ... but they also
knew that this would save the soul of the Irish
people...."
"Never did a group of people start on a more
desperate road with a cleaner conscience and
greater courage. They did it for Ireland's
soul."[11]

While ostensibly dwelling on the Irish Easter Rebellion
of 1916, Lechi was of course alluding to its own choice and
its own fate.   Earlier, in the Hanuka (Jewish Festival of
Lights, in memory of the Jewish Insurrection of the
Maccabees against the Greeks) issue of December 1940,
there was a "dated" essay on "Yehuda the Maccabee,"
written in 1884 by Eliezer Ben Yehuda, the resurrector of
the Hebrew language.   "The Maccabee's grandest exploit
was his death in battle with the enemy," writes Ben Yehuda,
and continues, "The valour of these heroes in their death ...
will strengthen the spirit of the Jew in our desperate
times...."[12]   He had in mind the period of pogroms in
Russia in the 1880's.   This mood corresponded to the spirit
of Yair's poem of 1934 where he writes:

And we shall believe in the day of the shadow of
   death
A time when the rifle will sing its battle-song.
We shall wrestle with God and with death and
   welcome Zion's redeemer.
We shall welcome him, Our blood will be a red
   carpet on the streets.
And upon this carpet--our brains, like white
   roses."[13]

By its desperate choice to fight against the government which implemented the White Paper of 1939, while the Jewish people were being slaughtered in Europe--and by making that choice in the face of an impossible dilemma-- Lechi became, as Eldad has expressed it, "not only the first to open the struggle against the British Government; not only the sole fighting underground which never put down its arms, not even for a single moment; but also the only group that saw the British as a foe and a foreign ruler, against whom war was imperative and imminent."[14] "Lechi," adds Eldad, "was also the first to make it clear that the struggle was not against this or that White Paper, but against the foreign rule itself which usurped the authority and published White Papers. Not against a 'bad' High-Commissioner, but against the very establishment of a foreign High-Commissioner, even if it were benevolent."[15]

This view, held by a tiny minority, was at that time, a crucial political and ideological turning point. Later, it became a generally accepted view, but only with the advent of the long-awaited and seemingly "friendly" Labor government in Britain, which rapidly betrayed all its previous commitments to Zionism and to the Jewish people. The tiny Lechi underground party, which decided to carry out its concept of 'fighting Zionism' by declaring war on the foreign ruler was soon beaten and almost liquidated. Isolated, despised, and persecuted, they were losing their best men in hopeless and futile clashes.

This ordeal brought about two cardinal changes in the character and methods of warfare of the Lechi underground. First came the inner structural and ideological transformation from a military underground organization into what they termed as an underground of revolutionaries. From soldiers of a hierarchical military body, subject to the authority of commanders, the Lechi fighter turned into a revolutionary, subject to loyalty to an ideal alone. The other crucial change consisted in the fact that Lechi abandoned its plans of armed military rebellion and abandoned even the idea of partisan warfare. They were too few and too weak. They now espoused acts of individual terror, as had been adopted in the past by Russian revolutionaries of the late 19th and the early 20th centuries--the Social Revolutionaries in particular. Another source of inspiration was that of the Polish Socialist Fighting Organization of 1904-1909, led at that time by Pilsudski, which resorted to what they termed "the armed deed." In the Lechi brochure of February 1944, dedicated to Yair, we find a passage of Yair's which points to his sources of inspiration: "A fighting body, a revolutionary organization does not have to, and cannot, attach itself to establishing institutions.... Did the Polish Fighting Organization have any, or did the Sinn Fein in Ireland ... or the Russian Social Revolutionaries have any?"[16]

Individual terror as a method was not chosen by formal decision but rather evolved by trial and error, as a fatal escalation, typical of many other revolutionary underground movements. In a letter of June 2, 1970, to Boyer-Bell, responding to a draft of Boyer-Bell's research on the FFI, Eldad writes, "You state that it was decided to use terrorist rather than guerrilla methods. This is simply not so. There was never such a decision. The fact that we chose this method was a direct consequence of the fact that we were so few ... as our numbers grew, we also resorted to guerrilla tactics."[17] If pressed to state my own position vis-a-vis this dilemma, I would argue that if there was no formal decision, there remained an ideological background to this choice. There was, as I have stated above, the Russian social-revolutionary example and the Irish and Polish revolutionary experiences.

In August 1943, we find in one of the first issues of *Hechazit (The Front)*, Lechi's ideological illegal organ, a programmatic article entitled "Terror," whose author remains unknown (despite all my efforts and investigations to establish his identity), which runs as follows:

> There was a time when 'the question of terror' was hotly debated in the land of revolutions--Russia-- but the period of those debates has long since receded into the past.... An argument can arise from an incorrect presentation of the question.

If the question is: Is it possible to start a
revolution or to bring about liberation by means of
terror?--the answer is NO! If the question is:
Do these actions help to bring revolution and
liberation nearer?--the answer is YES! ... First-
ly, terror is for us a part of contemporary political
warfare, and it plays a very large role. In
language which will be heard throughout the
world, even by our wretched brothers beyond the
borders of this land, it is proof of our war against
the occupier.... It is not aimed at persons, but at
representatives, and is therefore effective. And if
it also shakes the population out of its compla-
cency, so much the better. Thus, and for no other
reason, the battle for liberation will com-
mence."[18]

I find it helpful to cite this anonymous, directive
article because of its emphasis on adopting "individual
terror," which "is not aimed at persons, but at representatives." There lies the distinction between modern blind,
indiscriminate, and brutal terrorism--of the Palestinian or
Baader-Meinoff brand--and the individual terror of the
Russian Social Revolutionary brand, as adopted by Lechi.
In an essay entitled "Four Way of Struggle," by I.
Eldad, and published in No 4 of *The Deed*, March 1946, there
are repeated calls to attack the main arteries of the foreign
rule--the staff and the headquarters. He also states:
"We shall not shoot at innocent British civilians, at their
women and children.... We shall not attack British women
and children in the streets of London."[19] Again and again
this is the message, and it should be borne in mind that Eldad
was one of the most extreme and radical of the Lechi
leaders. In his aforementioned letter to Boyer-Bell, Eldad
also refers to the question of the moral justification of
"individual terror." He writes, "In justification of individual acts of terror against central figures of the administration we frequently raised the question of whether history
itself might not have been changed if only, between 1933
and 1939, someone had succeeded in assassinating

Hitler."20   A similar argument was also raised by the left-wing Lechi leader Yelin Mor, when he was interviewed by a London *Thames* Television journalist in 1977.   When asked if he found revolutionary violence of the kind used by Lechi justifiable, he retorted that he did not know of the history of any nation that had achieved its freedom without resorting to violence.   Yet, the brand of violence that Lechi had used was more justifiable and more moral because it had concentrated on objects and on persons who were directly or indirectly responsible for the crimes perpetrated.   If, at the close of World War II, he told the journalist, you had been forced to choose between assassinating the Mikado or dropping the atom bomb, you would surely have chosen to assassinate the Mikado.21

In his brilliant and reliable work on the history of Lechi, Yelin Mor talks about his meetings in the underground with Eliahu Golomb, head of the Hagana. When Eliahu Golomb had posed the question about why Lechi had resorted to such drastic actions as the assassination of Lord Moyne, or the repeated attempt on the life of the High-Commissioner, Sir Harold MacMichael, Yelin Mor's reply was, "In our view the political impact of an action-of-war is the product of two factors: the extent of the fighting force, and the intensity of the action."   He meant that if one had a larger fighting force, its operations would not need to be so dramatic or so intensive. Continuing, he said, "We are a small group in comparison with the Hagana, and therefore our actions have to be spectacular and intensive."22   There is another element which distinguishes Lechi's principle of 'individual terror' from the brutality of modern, indiscriminate terrorism.   To make this distinction clear, an example will best serve the purpose.   Camus, in his book *The Rebel*, in which he attempts to point out where the limits of terror lie, can arrive at no clearcut doctrinal solution but resorts, instead, to an example chosen from the history of the Russian Social Revolutionaries.   Ivan Kaliayev refused to throw his bomb at the carriage of the Grand Prince Sergei because he had noticed at the critical moment that it was occupied by an innocent   woman   and   her   children.   Later   Kaliayev succeeded at a second attempt, which, unlike the first attempt, occurred at such a time when his presence was so conspicuous that his attack was rendered suicidal.[23]

One can point out in the history of Lechi numerous examples of this kind. One of them, recently disclosed, involves Yehoshua Cohen, among the boldest and most representative Lechi leaders, later to become Ben-Gurion's closest friend at Sde Boker. On January 20, 1942, a dangerous and vital assignment was entrusted to Yehoshua Cohen, namely, the elimination of two brutal and much hated heads of the Jewish Department of the British CID: Morton and Wilkin. Neither time, energy, nor sophisticated planning had been spared for this operation. In the instructions which he received and accepted, Yehoshua Cohen was ordered to carry out the attempt by any means, even at the cost of his own life. Then, as he was about to detonate the explosion, following a previous explosion which had served as a snare, Yehoshua noticed that numerous innocent bystanders were assembled at the target area for the blast. He felt that he could not accomplish his assignment and so cause their wanton deaths. Risking his own life, he then withdrew and did not carry out the commission. Forty years later, when this could all be brought to light, he said that it had been one of the hardest decisions of his life; but were he to be presented once again with a situation of this nature, he would have again chosen the same path. In fact, Wilkin and Morton, whose lives were spared by Yehoshua's split-second decision guided by his conscience, later personally killed unarmed Lechi prisoners; and it was Morton who murdered Yair, leader of Lechi.[24]

There were two predominant factors inherent in this kind of warfare which determined what I would term its moral limits. One was the direction and planning from the center. Here I shall cite Yitzhak Shamir. In his speech to the Fighters' Conference of April 1949, when someone accused him of excessive concentration of power in the Lechi Center, he retorted, "If there was in fact an excessive concentration of power, and if we did sometimes watch carefully over everyone's moves, and often clipped overzealous wings, there were serious reasons for doing so. You should remember that we started after failures which were caused by anarchy, and by many a desire to act independently; and terrible catastrophies befell us on this account."25   Individual terror had to be carefully planned, watched, and directed.   On the other hand, there was a second factor inherent in this method of struggle, namely the individual fighters' decision, which as can be seen from the example of Yehoshua Cohen, was indeed sometimes crucial.   The fact that the moral standard of most Lechi fighters was exceptionally high served as a safeguard that the delicate, thin line of moral limits would not be overstepped.

When Eliahu Hakim, one of the two Lechi assassins of Lord Moyne, was already out of danger, he noticed that his comrade Eliahu Betzuri had been wounded and caught.   No instructions, no previous planning could have guided him how to act in this split-second—he made his own decision. He returned from his position of safety to help Betzuri and to share his lot with him—together they went to the gallows.26   This illustrates yet again that thin line that distinguished the Lechi fighters from the indiscriminate, cold-blooded terrorists of the modern ilk.   The Lechi fighter would resort to a violence that he hated, knowing as he did so, its limits and its moral risks.   In this sense he could be seen as following in the tradition of the Social Revolutionaries of Russia and of their leader Grigori Gershuni, who, in a bitter dispute with Lenin once contended, "Only a revolutionary party which does not breach the revolutionary morality—the highest morality to be implemented in life—only such a party contains the force of life.   A socialist party can win only by moral integrity and not by physical predominance."26   On another occasion Gershuni stated: "Means that do not befit the aim can pervert the aim forever, and this being so, terror must be treated as a drug, that while it can cure, may also kill.... Only one who has mastered the anguish of terror and revolution, only he who knows the moral contradictions inherent in them, is armed against slipping and falling."27

Yelin Mor stated his intentions towards the Yishuv (the Jewish community in the land of Israel), as: "We desire to be the catalyst, the accelerator of the historical process, until the majority of our people will stand up in arms to fight foreign rule." On another occasion, meeting the Hagana leaders--Eliahu Golomb, Israel Galili, and Moshe Sneh--in April 1945, Yelin Mor declared on behalf of Lechi that Lechi was ready to dissolve its separate organizational existence and carry on as an ideological faction only if the Hagana would offer an activist-Zionist line of action in which Lechi members could be given an outlet for their determination to fight. Thus, he did in fact predict the future.[28]

The State of Israel emerged out of the common struggle of the three underground movements. Although they had come into conflict and often even confronted one another, they did finally, by a fortunate turn of fate which Hegel would have called "the cunning of history," in fact complement one another. When Lechi had fulfilled its historical destiny there was no longer any need for its separate existence; and though many of its members deplored the fact vehemently, Lechi merged into the varied political fabric of Israel.

<hr>

NOTES

1. "Sulam," No 4, February 1962, p 5 (in Hebrew).
2. The First Conference of the Fighters, March 1949, Ramat-Gan: Publ. 'The Fighter's Party,' p 39.
3. *Ma'ariv* newspaper, February 3, 1967, pp 7,8.
4. Avraham Stern (Yair), *Collected Poems* (in Hebrew), 4th ed., 1976, p 19.
5. *History of the Hagana* (in Hebrew), 'Am-Oved' publishers, Tel Aviv, 1973, pp 9-11.
6. Victor Serge: *Memoirs of a Revolutionary*, London, 1953, pp 1,2.
7. Op. cit: 'Undser Welt,' Warsaw, September 23, 1938, (in Yiddish), *History of the Hagana*.
8. *History of the Hagana*, Vol III, op. cit., pp 20-21.

9. August 1941, illegal transmission, Lohamey Herut Israel (Fighters for Freedom of Israel), *Collected Works*, Vol I, Tel Aviv, 1959, p 91.

10. *Ibid.*, pp 91-94.

11. cited in *In the Underground*, No 5, February 1941, "Lechi," *Collected Works*, op. cit., Vol I, pp 53-55.

12. cited in *In the Underground*, No 3, December 1941, "Lechi," *Collected Works*, Vol I, p 38.

13. Yair, *Poems*, (in Hebrew), op. cit., p 33.

14. *Sulam*, monthly, cit. 1962, pp 29-32.

15. Israel Eldad, 'Ma'aser Rishon' ('The First Tithe') (in Hebrew), 3rd ed., 1976, Tel Aviv, pp 107-108.

16. Yair, *Lechi: Collected Works*, Vol I, pp 397-398; see also *Lechi: Collected Works*, op. cit.

17. I. Eldad. Letter to Boyer-Bell of June 2, 1970.

18. 'Hachazit,' ('The Front'), July 1943, "Terror," Lechi *Collected Works*, Vol I, op. cit., pp 141-144.

19. 'Hamaas,' ('The Deed'), No 4, February 1946, *Lechi: Collected Works*, Vol II, pp 99-100.

20. *Ibid.*, I. Eldad, letter to Boyer-Bell, June 2, 1970.

21. Interview with Yelin Mor, on January 19, 1978.

22. Nathan Yelin Mor, *Lechi: People, Ideas and Deeds*, Tel Aviv, 1974, pp 237-238.

23. Albert Camus, *The Rebel*, London, 1967, Penguin, pp 248-251.

24. See *Wanted* by Y. Eliav, Jerusalem, 1983 (in Hebrew), pp 194-207. See also *Ma'ariv*.

25. "The Fighters' Conference," 1949, op. cit., p 39.

26. N. Yelin Mor, *Lechi: People, Ideas and Deeds*, op. cit., pp 220-221.

27. V. Chernov, *Grigori Gershuni* (in Yiddish), ed. Workmens' Circle, New York, 1934, pp 33-34. See also Zeev Ivianski, "The Moral Issue--Some Aspects of Individual Terror," *The Morality of Terrorism*, Pergamon Press, ed. D.C. Rappoport, Yonah Alexander; New York, 1982, pp 229-266.

28. N. Yelin Mor, *Lechi: People, Ideas and Deeds*, pp 245, 263.

PART FOUR
THIRD WORLD PERSPECTIVE

CHAPTER VIII

The Middle East Experience

Professor M. Maoz

On February 3, 1982, armed squads of the Muslim Brothers' underground organization launched a surprise attack on government headquarters in the city of Hama, a traditionally Muslim conservative town, situated on the main road between Damascus and Aleppo. They stormed offices of the security services, the police, and the Ba'th party, and executed some 250 officers and officials including the governor as well as local activists of the Ba'th and communist parties. Holding the entire city for several days, these Muslim rebels called for a nationwide popular uprising and a holy war (Jihad) against the "atheist" regime of the Ba'th, presumably having in mind the model of the Islamic revolution in Iran of February 1979. However, the powerful Ba'th regime of President Hafez Assad did not delay its reaction: armored units shelled the city, destroying many of its buildings including ancient mosques, and indiscriminately killing many thousands of citizens-- men, women, and children. The brutal suppression of the Hama revolt marked the culmination of the violent conflict between the Muslim opposition and the Ba'th regime, which had started following the Ba'th coup d'etat, or revolution of March 1963.

HISTORICAL BACKGROUND

For generations prior to the Ba'th takeover, Syrian socio-political life had been greatly influenced by the country's large Sunni-Muslim conservative population and its powerful Muslim-religious leadership, the 'Ulama. Drawing on the allegiance and support of their religious followers, these leaders struggled in various ways-- including violent measures against government attempts at modernization which damaged or threatened to erode the Islamic character of the state as well as the socio-political status and economic interests of those religious leaders. For example, Muslim conservative and fanatic elements led by 'Ulama fiercely opposed the attempts of the Ottoman-Turkish government in the mid-19th century to reform the Islamic-oriented legal system and to grant equal rights to the Christian and Jewish minorities in the country. These Muslim elements carried out a pogrom in Aleppo in 1850 and a massacre in Damascus in 1860 against the local Christians who had insisted upon obtaining their new rights.[1] Likewise, during the period of the French mandate in Syria, Muslim 'Ulama successfully fought against the clauses of the newly promulgated constitution of 1930 which provided for freedom of religion and conscience and equal rights to all citizens.[2]

THE MUSLIM BROTHERS (AL-IKHWAN AL-MUSLIMMUN)

Prior to the Ba'th revolution these conservative elements--the 'Ulama and the traditional Muslim urban middle and lower classes--constituted the social milieu of the Muslim Brothers, an organization which was established in Syria toward the end of the 1930s. Based on the teaching and model of the Muslim Brothers in Egypt,[3] this organization operated under various names such as "Shabab Muhammad" (Muhammad's Youth); its political positions were voiced by several "independent" politicians or by members of different nationalist parties. In the 1947 national elections, following Syria's independence, three

Muslim Brothers representatives and followers were elected to the parliament; in 1954, five of those were represented in the Parliament, and following the 1961 elections ten Ikhwan members and followers held seats in the Syrian Parliament (out of 150 members). Significantly, among their supporters were General Nahlawi, the leader of the 1961 coup, and Dr. Dawalibi, Syria's Prime Minister in the early 1960s. Yet the chief spiritual and political leaders of the Ikhwan at that period were members of the 'Ulama--Sheikh Mustafa al-Siba'i, the first leader, during the 1940s and 1950s; Sheikh 'Isam al-'Attar, the leader during the 1960s; followed by Sheikh Marwan Hadid, the leader in the late 1960s. Until the Ba'th takeover in March 1963, this fundamentalist Islamic movement operated legally and openly struggled against new measures taken by reformist or leftist rulers directed to abolish or weaken Islamic institutions or customs in the country.[4] The chief methods of their struggle were extra-parliamentary, namely: public strikes, demonstrations, and disturbances.

MUSLIM OPPOSITION TO THE BA'TH REGIME

The ascendancy of the Ba'th regime in Syria opened a new and crucial era of brutal conflict between the conservative or fundamentalist Islamic forces and the new rulers of the country. This conflict continued in several dimensions. First, the Ba'th regime carried out, for the first time, a far-reaching policy aimed at diminishing the role of Islam in public life, and in effect separating Islam from the state. This secularist policy was manifested inter alia in the reduction of religious teachings (both Muslim and Christian) in government schools, and in constraining the functions of various religious institutions. In addition to anti-Islamic and atheist expressions in the official media, the neo-Ba'th regime under Salah Jadid (1966-1970) erased the Islamic clauses from the Syrian constitution. It also violently suppressed Muslim anti-government demonstrations causing bloodshed, shelling of mosques, and arresting of scores of religious leaders.

A second related factor which contributed to both expanding and deepening the antagonism of the Muslim population toward the Ba'th regime, was the ascendency of the 'Alawi minority in 1966 to the foci of power in Syria. While a large part of the orthodox Sunni-Muslims have regarded the Alawis (12 percent of the population) as heretics, many others have looked down at the Alawis as a socially and culturally inferior community. Thus, the Alawi military rule in Syria for the first time in history, coupled with the secularist tendencies of its regime, have created feelings of bitterness, frustration, and animosity among large sections of the Sunni-Muslim majority. And if these two factors were not sufficient causes for the Sunni-Alawi conflict, two other grievances created an overflow of hatred and antagonism, particularly among the Muslim urban population: the brutal repression of basic human, legal, and political rights; and the strict socialist reforms which hit the socio-economic interests of the upper class as well as the traditional middle classes of the Muslim population.

Yet these Muslim sections of the Syrian population have been unable since 1963 to express their complaints and frustrations by means of political parties. All veteran Syrian parties, except for the Ba'th, the communist, and two small socialist parties, were outlawed by the Ba'th regime. Consequently, the only socio-political movement which could serve as an opposition center to the regime was that of the Muslim Brothers, which formed an underground organization. Becoming the focus of Sunni-Muslim defiance to the government, the Ikhwan (or Muslim Brothers) both attracted the allegiance and manifested the antagonism of many Syrian Muslims. In their struggle against the Ba'th regime, the Ikhwan utilized the large "network" of many hundreds of mosques and 'Ulama, propagating their pro-Islamic and anti-government teachings.[5] Throughout the period of the Ba'th rule, the Ikhwan initiated, organized, and directed many public demonstrations, disturbances, and other actions of civil disobedience against the regime in the main cities of Syria. They fired at army units, assassinated military officers and cadets, and even attempted to kill president Hafiz al Assad in 1981.

HAFIZ AL ASSAD VERSUS
THE MUSLIM OPPOSITION

President Assad, a cool, cautious, and pragmatic leader, endeavoured for several years after his ascendancy in 1970 to mitigate popular opposition and appease the various sections of the Sunni-Muslim population.6 He reintroduced the Islamic clauses in the Syrian constitution, lifted the previous restrictions on religious teachings, and distributed public honors and government appointments to Sunni-Muslim 'Ulama. Assad also encouraged the construction of new mosques and made various gestures to present himself as a devout Muslim. Simultaneously, Assad tried to conciliate the traditional Muslim middle classes which had been affected by the economic reforms of Salah Jadid. He modified the socialistic measures of his predecessor, lifted restrictions on the import of consumer goods, encouraged economic activity, and private initiative. For several years these gestures and actions partly neutralized the Muslim opposition to the regime particularly during and following the 1973 war against Israel. The Yom Kippur War gave Assad an opportunity to demonstrate his alleged adherence to Islam and the war was declared a Holy War (Jihad) against the "enemies of Islam".

Yet in the long run even a seasoned and shrewd politician like Assad was unable to bridge the huge gap, or cover over the deep structural conflict between the regime and its followers on the one hand, and large sections of the Sunni-Muslim population on the other. In order to maintain his regime, Assad has had to lean upon the military support of his Alawi comrades, and to grant them special economic and political privileges. Simultaneously, however, Assad has attempted to broaden the social support base of his regime by winning the allegiance of other groups among the Syrian population. Thus, apart from other minorities such as the Druze and the Christians, who were granted special attention, large sections within the Muslim community have become the beneficiaries of the Ba'th reforms:

- any of the peasants (some 60 percent of the Syrian population) were granted land, credit, and tractors under the laws of agrarian reforms.
- The workers saw their standard of living and social security greatly improved under the Ba'th regime.
- The young intelligentsia were educated free of cost in government schools and universities and thereafter received appointments in the state and public administration.

By contrast, large sections of the urban Muslim population--the traditional upper and middle classes, modern entrepreneurs, and professionals--were, or felt themselves, deprived of their socio-economic interests. Many of these poeple also resented the military-sectarian character of the regime, its secularist anti-Islamic tendencies as well as its repressive measures. Consequently, the struggle of the Muslim opposition against the Ba'th regime, which initially had been guided and led by 'Ulama using Islamic slogans and traditional methods of resistance, has significantly changed in character and tactics since the mid-1970s. The new leaders of the Ikhwan, now called Mujahidun (Holy Warriors), such as Adnan Sad al-Din and his successor Adnan Uqla, like other active members of the organization, were not only drawn from the 'Ulama but also from the class of professionals-- engineers, doctors, lawyers, etc. Apart from the traditional Islamic motifs, these leaders now employ notions of democracy, freedom, rule, and law in their appeals to the population to resist the Ba'th regime.[7] Warfare tactics of the Mujahidun since the mid-1970s were not only confined to street demonstrations and other actions of civil disobedience and many of their members were trained in commando fighting in bases in Jordan, Lebanon, and elsewhere. In the last several years they have carried out a series of bold guerrilla operations against military and government targets using arms acquired abroad and causing heavy losses and embarrassment to the Assad's regime.

Yet, these commando or terrorist activities of the Muslim opposition, however daring and sophisticated, have by no means succeeded in overthrowing the Ba'th regime. It is also unlikely that such guerrilla warfare stands any chance to cause the downfall of Assad's regime, brutal counter-terror by the regime is one reason. The regime has caused bloodshed among the Muslim resistance, for instance, in the Hama incident in February 1982 which possibly served to curtail and deter further anti-government sabotage. A more crucial reason for the inability of the Islamic terrorists in Syria to topple the Ba'th rule is that this powerful regime controls the centers of power in the country--a huge and strong military force, and effective security services which are by and large loyal to Assad. Unlike the 1979 revolutionary situation in Iran, growing sections of the Syrian population--Ba'th members, the public bureaucracy, young intelligentsia, workers, and peasants--all identify with or support the Ba'th regime of Assad, or have developed vested interests in its survival.

NOTES

1. Moshe Maoz, *Ottoman Reform in Syria and Palestine* (Oxford), Ch. 5.
2. Cf. League of Nations, Report of the Permanent Mandate Commission, 27th Session, A.H. Hourani, *Minorities in the Arab World* (OUP 1947), p 77.
3. For a comprehensive study see, R.P. Mitchell, *The Society of the Muslim Brothers* (OUP 1969); also Ishak Musa Husaini, *The Moslem Brethren* (Beirut 1956).
4. See for example P. Seale, *The Struggle for Syria* (OUP 1965), p 121. On the Muslim Brothers in Syria between 1947 and 1952, see S. Reissner *Ideologie und Politik der Muslimbruder Syriens* (Freiburg, 1980).
5. For details see Hanna Batatu "Syria's Muslim Brethren" *MERIP Reports* (1982), pp 12-20; A. Drysdade, "The Asad Regime and its Troubles," *Idem*, pp 3-11; U.F. Abd-allah, *The Islamic Struggle in Syria* (Berkeley, 1983).
6. See Moshe Maoz, "Hafiz al Asad: A Political Profile," *The Jerusalem Quarterly* (8, 1978), pp 16-31.
7. Batatu, "Syria's Muslim Brethren," p 13.

CHAPTER IX

Terrorists and Guerrillas in Africa

J. Lisker

The Subcommittee on Security and Terrorism was established during the 97th Congress in January 1981 by Senator Strom Thurmond, Chairman of the Judiciary Committee. He selected Senator Denton to serve as its chairman.

During the 97th Congress, and the 1st session of the 98th Congress, the Subcommitte held 40 hearings dealing with national security matters, including those held in the exercise of Subcommittee oversight of the FBI. In early 1982, the Subcommittee held a particularly revealing set of hearings on the activities of Cuban agents in the U.S. The hearings underscored the involvement of the Soviet Union in southern Africa and Latin America, and Cuba's able execution of its role as Moscow's surrogate. Because of the economic and strategic importance of southern Africa to the United States and to the free world, we concluded that the Subcommittee should turn its attention to the Soviet, Cuban, and East German involvement in the terrorist activities of the so-called "National Liberation Movements" in southern Africa.

In reaching this conclusion, we took into account the fact that many journalists and opinion leaders throughout the world are frequently reluctant to admit or even discuss the extent of communist involvement and control of southern African "liberation movements." But motivated by the conviction that African blacks, as well as whites, will suffer as communist movements expand or triumph in that region, and mindful of the impact on American interest of such a development, we went ahead. Preparation for the series of hearings commenced with an extensive program of study undertaken by the Subcommittee staff on the antecedents, creation, and development of the major "liberation movements" of southern Africa. On the basis of this preliminary study, we decided to focus the Subcommittee's further inquiry on two organizations, the African National Congress of South Africa (ANC) and the South West Africa People's Organization (SWAPO). To that end the Subcommittee went to South Africa and Namibia where the staff interviewed a number of potential witnesses, many of whom had been trained in insurgency and terrorist activity in the Soviet Union and in the German Democratic Republic (GDR). From the large number of potential ANC and SWAPO witnesses, we selected 8 who had ANC connections, and 4 who had SWAPO connections. In addition, we heard the testimony of expert witnesses such as Chester Crocker, Assistant Secretary of State for African Affairs, and Dr. Peter Vanneman, a Sovietologist from the University of Arkansas.

On March 22, 1982, the Subcommittee on Security and Terrorism, commenced the hearings on the role of the Soviet Union, Cuba, and East Germany in fomenting terrorism in southern Africa. In order to reach its conclusion the Subcommittee, in addition to hearing testimony, also studied many hundreds of documents, some of which were printed into the record of the hearing which comprises nearly 2,000 pages. The Subcommittee concluded in its report based on the hearings that the USSR, the GDR, and others have infiltrated the ranks of these two principal political African organizations and that they are openly assisting the ANC and SWAPO in the use of terror tactics in order to achieve certain political objectives.

Senator Denton made it clear at the outset that the Subcommittee on Security and Terrorism was not the appropriate forum to debate what U.S. policy should be towards southern Africa, nor was it the appropriate forum to analyze South African domestic policy. The Senator, however, stated very clearly what the Subcommittee's attitude was towards racial discrimination:

> Surely, no one on this Subcommittee would condone or attempt to justify, in any respect, policies of racial discrimination in South Africa, the United States or elsewhere.

U.S. policy makers concerned with southern Africa are therefore faced with a most difficult dilemma, which I believe these hearings through its deliberations and findings have clearly defined. On the one hand, there is the South African government, democratically elected by the white minority, whose racial policies are repugnant to the moral values upon which the United States of America is based. On the other hand, there are the so-called liberation movements of which the ANC is the most important. Founded in 1912 as a purely black nationalist movement with its prime objective the securing of political rights for the black majority, it has become in the course of years, as these hearings clearly demonstrated, a front organization for the South African Communist Party. With the full support of the Soviet Union and its allies, it has resorted to terrorism in order to achieve its political ends.

Leaving aside, for the moment the fact that the ANC is an organization dominated by communists, the dilemma facing U.S. policy makers and the American people is whether to support a self-styled national liberation organization which openly espouses violence in its quest for political power. In my view it is regrettable that there is a strong body of opinion in the U.S. and elsewhere that the ANC is worthy of our support. Senator Denton put it very eloquently as follows:

Some well-intentioned persons argue that the failure of Western governments to support reformist or radical elements in developing societies that, confronted with social, political, or economic inequity, attempt to achieve their goals by force, drives them into the arms of the Soviets. According to this school of thought, the proper course for the United States is to be supportive of these radical elements and their general goal in order to preempt Soviet support. I wish it were so simple. In reality, of course, right and wrong are rarely so clearly differentiated in human society that the choices are obvious or easy.

We in the United States pride ourselves as being a civilized society. Our Republic is firmly rooted in the idea that the grievances of its citizens are addressed in open and public debate. No matter how fiercely controversies may rage, the lives and property of all are protected by law. Therefore, just as we cannot condone violence to solve problems at home, we cannot condone violence in solving problems abroad, and should we become involved in supporting the violence, we threaten the very fabric of our society. If we support the ANC or SWAPO, then in principle, there is nothing preventing us from supporting the IRA or the PLO or any other terrorist organization.

In southern Africa the question of whether the U.S. should support the ANC or SWAPO is complicated by the presence of the Soviets in these organizations. It is clear that the Soviet involvement is not as a result of helping an oppressed people in achieving their rights, as the Soviet record in this regard falls somewhat short of perfection. Assistant Secretary of State Dr. Crocker pointed out South Africa is a mineral-rich country accounting for over 40 percent of Sub-Saharan African GNP, for 70 percent of its industrial and 60 percent of its mining output, 80 percent of the steel and 85 percent of the electricity consumed. As far as strategic interests are concerned, Dr. Crocker pointed out that 86 percent of the world's platinum reserves are in South Africa; 53 percent of the world's manganese reserves, 64 percent of vanadium, 95 percent of chromium, 52 percent cobalt, a "dominant share of world gold and diamond output, and internationally significant amounts of coal, uranium, copper, and other minerals." Dr. Crocker contends that "many of these minerals are vital to Western defense and high technology industries ..." In addition, the Cape sea route is vital to the NATO alliance. It is estimated that 2,300 ships travel that route each month delivering 57 percent of Western Europe's imported oil and 20 percent of the United State's imported oil. Some 70 percent of strategic raw materials used by NATO are transported via the Cape route. In September 1980, General Alexander Haig, in his capacity as President and Chief Executive officer of United Technologies Corporation, testified before the Subcommittee of Mines, and Mining of the Committee on Interior and Insular Affairs in the House of Representatives:

> The United States is inordinately and increasingly dependent on foreign sources of supply for many of the raw materials critical to our defense and our economy ... Should future trends, especially in southern Africa, result in alignment with Moscow of this critical resource area, then the USSR will control as much as 90 percent of several key minerals for which no substitutes have been developed, and the loss of which could bring the severest consequences to the existing economic and security framework of the free world.

One of the witnesses who testified before the Subcommittee, Dr. Peter Vanneman, an Associate Professor of Political Science at the University of Arkansas, stated:

> The USSR is striving to enhance its influence in southern Africa not merely to affect events there but to influence events throughout the continent and the world. Its purpose is not merely to dominate the southern African region, but to utilize its influence there to enhance its influence elsewhere.

A publication by the University of California Press entitled, *South Africa: Time Running Out*, sums up the points rather well. The following is stated:

- A variety of motives have been advanced for the Soviet Union's involvement in southern Africa.
- It hopes to stake out a role for itself in the ultimate denouncement of the racial conflict in the region, thereby reinforcing its claims to status as a global power.
- It seeks to promote the emergence of Soviet-leaning radical black governments in the area. It has already achieved a measure of success in Angola and Mozambique and hopes for eventual success in Namibia and South Africa.
- It seeks to win local acceptance of a Soviet political, economic, and military presence. Among its economic interests is access to the area's minerals. Although the USSR itself possesses enough reserves of the minerals southern Africa has to offer to make it essentially self-sufficient, it faces additional demands on its supplies from other Communist nations, particularly those in Eastern Europe. Besides the supplying of arms and advisers, its military links have included arrangements permitting Soviet warships to call at local ports and Soviet reconnaissance planes to use local airfields.
- It would like to see a weakening of the Western position in the region, not only politically but also economically and strategically. The USSR, some analysts assert, has an interest in impeding Western access to the minerals in the area and in disrupting Western use of the sea lanes around the Cape. Commenting on Africa as a whole, a Soviet analyst said in 1980:

> Despite all efforts undertaken by the United States, the main tendency consists in the gradual weakening of the positions of the leading Western powers on the Continent. With the material and

moral-political support of the socialist community, the African people are inflicting one defeat after another on imperialism.

At this juncture I will attempt to summarize and to analyze the testimony which led to the inevitable conclusion that the ANC and SWAPO are communist inspired terrorist movements.   I would hasten to add that while the evidence produced at the hearings which is now part of the public record does not permit us to judge the Soviet Union guilty of direct responsibility for choosing terrorist targets or exercising detailed supervision over terrorist operations, it should be clear that the Soviets and their proxies do instigate, train and supply a variety of terrorist groups. The conclusion is therefore inescapable that were it not for this support, the terrorist epidemic of the 1970s and 1980s certainly would not have risen to the present levels of barbarity.

THE ANC

South Africa's racial policies are deeply rooted in its past.   This fact is not offered as an apology but must be borne in mind in order to understand the racial conflict which has embittered the lives of so many South Africans-- black and white alike.   Serious efforts were never made in the past to weld the various races in South Africa into one nation.   In fact, the policy of the colonial powers was quite the opposite.   At the same time it must also be said that there is no evidence that the blacks sought to integrate with the whites.   In 1909, when the British Government agreed to a union of the four provinces resulting in the formation of the Union of South Africa in 1910 as an independent autonomous state within the British Commonwealth of Nations, it could have insisted in creating and safeguarding political and civil rights of all of its citizens irrespective of race, color, or religious affiliation.

It chose not to do so.   Accordingly, on January 8, 1912, the ANC was founded in Bloemfontein.   Roland Stanbridge, a researcher at the Scandanavian Institute of

African Studies in Uppsala, Sweden, describes its creation as follows:

> When Britain handed political power in South Africa over to the privileged white minority in 1910, Africans throughout the country were faced with the need to unite to protect their rights. A prominent Zulu lawyer, Dr. Pixley ka Isaka Seme, declared in 1922: The demon of racism, the aberrations of Xhosa-Fingo feuds, the animosity that exists between the Zulu and the Tongas, between the Basuto and every other native, must be buried and forgotten ... We are one people. Other overseas-trained, professional men took up the call, and on January 8, 1912, the founding conference of the ANC (at first called the Native National Congress) opened in Bloemfontein. Its purpose, as set forth in Seme's opening address, was to find ways and means of forming one national union for the purpose of creating national unity and defending our rights and privileges.

Jordan K. Ngubane in his book *An African Explains Apartheid*, has commented as follows about the political goals of the founders of the ANC:

> After lengthy and careful deliberation, the delegates agreed to unite their peoples for the purpose of projecting them into the future as a new politico-cultural community. They were no longer to be narrowly Zulu or Xhosa or Satu; they were going to be the African people. Their unity was designed to extend the area of liberty; to give to citizenship the same meaning on both sides of the color line, and not to drive the Indian, colored, or white man into the sea. Thirdly, the delegates regarded the violation of human rights by the Union Government's race policy as a matter that concerned humanity as a whole. They rejected the contention that it was a domestic South African matter.

Stanbridge commented that in the aftermath of several decades of largely unsuccessful petitioning of successive Union governments by the ANC in support of (black) African rights, that closer cooperation began to develop between the forces opposed to the white government. For example, in 1944-1945 there was a widespread ANC-CP (South African Community Party) anti-pass campaign which did much to renew support for the ANC. Close fraternal relations developed between the ANC and CP and today the two organizations continue to work together intimately. After carefully reviewing the history of the ANC through the writings of scholars, the Subcommittee concluded that the ANC received scant recognition from successive South African governments. In fact, it received one setback after another. It remained, however, a political movement dedicated to the ideal of political change by peaceful means. However, in the 1940s this began to change. In 1943, a group of young intellectuals formed the ANC Youth League. As was pointed out by Stanbridge, "They propounded a policy of fighting for Africa's independence, freedom from domination by other national groups and the establishment of an African nation. An important dimension of the Youth League's outlook was the insistence that the ANC should cease merely making representations to a stubborn government and should engage in more militant action. It rejected the language of supplication of the ANC leadership." However, it would be wrong to say that the Youth League in the 1940s had decided upon violence as a political weapon; but its patience with the white government was beginning to wear thin.

Mention must be made of two other factors, namely the Communist Party and the electoral victory of the National Party in 1948. The South African Communist Party came into being in 1921 and exists to this day with offices in London. The communists saw in the Youth League a ready-made vehicle for capturing the ANC. Mr. Ngubane describes this as follows:

As soon as the [Second World] war was over, the [Youth] League intensified its pressure for a definite stand against race oppression. Although the resistance movement of 1951 was launched in time, the long debates which preceded this demonstration are perhaps more interesting, for the Youth Leaguers regarded the campaign primarily as a tactical move to train the African masses in the use of peaceful collective action. Some of them selected this weapon for reasons of principle, but others said that expediency had decided the issue for them. At first, the Communists dismissed the idea of a nonviolent demonstration; but when it became clear that African opinion supported the resistance campaign, the line changed. They were heart and soul for a Gandhian campaign. In the meantime, they had worked hard behind the scenes to create a coordinating committee representing all the organizations behind the campaign. The acceptance of equal representation on it by the Johannesburg Youth Leaguers, who were coming increasingly under the influence of the Communist leader, Dr. Yussuf Dadoo, imposed severe strains inside the League. After the campaign, however, Communist pressure on Youth League unity was intensified. Walter Sisulu, Duma Nokwe, and other Youth Leaguers visited Iron Curtain countries with disastrous effects on Youth League unity. The consequent tensions led finally to the capture of the League by the Communists. And that was its end.

It has been argued that the electoral victory of Dr. Malan's National Party in 1948, espousing as it did the policy of apartheid, facilitated the infiltration of the ANC by the Communist Party. This is an argument devoid of understanding of the factual situation as it existed in South Africa in 1948. The truth of the matter is that the National Party was merely saying out loud what its opponents were, in fact, practicing. The predecessors of Dr. Malan, as pointed out, also did not seek to integrate all of South

Africa's citizens into one nation. There was talk that General Jan Smuts was considering granting more political rights to Indians and Coloreds, but he clearly was not considering a policy of universal suffrage. But it cannot be denied that by openly espousing the policy of apartheid the National Party intensified black opposition. As the opposition began expressing itself in public demonstrations, strikes, and open hostility to the regime, the white Parliament responded by passing laws to deal with the situation. This led to public trials where blacks were prosecuted on charges of high treason and other statutory crimes pursuant to the provisions of the Suppression of Communism Act, the Sabotage Act, and the Terrorism Act. In addition, black leaders were banned and placed under house arrest; for example, Chief Luthuli, a Nobel Peace Prize winner, was forbidden to move outside the boundaries of the magisterial district in which he resided. These measures were harsh by any standard and were opposed by many within the Nationalist Party. The political opposition and the English press certainly objected. No purpose is to be served by discussing in any detail the measures the South African Government took in order to stifle black opposition. Suffice to say that those measures were harsh and caused a great deal of hardship, and it is regrettable that these laws remain to this day on the South Arican Statute book. But it must be borne in mind that the ANC at that time was already largely dominated by the South African Communist Party, having as its objective the overthrow of the government by violence, if all other measures were to fail, and to replace it with a Communist dictatorship. The Subcommittee, in fact, found that the ANC had become the front of the Communist Party.

It should be noted that the leadership of both the ANC and SWAPO were invited to testify. Mr. Sam Nujoma President of SWAPO did not respond and the head of the ANC observer mission at the U.N. simply advised the Chairman of the Subcommittee that the invitation had been relayed to ANC headquarters for a decision. No further response was received at that time.

We need do no more than to refer to a speech delivered by Oliver Tambo, the Secretary-General of the ANC, on the occasion of the 60th anniversary of the South African Communist Party, July 30, 1981.   This speech was published in *African Communist*, No 87, fourth quarter 1981, and in *Sechaba*, the official organ of the ANC, September 1981. Mr. Tambo has always denied being a member of the South African Communist Party and I am not aware of any direct evidence that he is a member; however, under his leadership the ANC clearly advanced the Moscow line as his speech indicated.   This is what he said:

> Comrade   Chairman,   Your   Excellencies,   and Comrades, Let me commence by thanking you, Comrade Chairman, and the SACP for inviting the African National Congress to be a party to this occasion and in particular, for the opportunity of sharing a platform with the Communist Party of Great Britain, represented here by the General Secretary Gordon McLennan and with the Communist Party of Ireland, represented by Comrade Michael O'Riordan.
> These are our allies; they are part of the international movement of solidarity which gives us strength and confidence in the certainty of our victory. These parties, together with other communist and workers parties around the world, are parties which we can always appeal to for solidarity in the conviction that they will respond.
> It is a great pleasure for us, a great honor to participate with them on an occasion of great significance in our struggle in South Africa.

That the ANC is a terrorist organization cannot now be denied.   In 1958, the African nationalist faction in the ANC, no longer willing to accept the domination of the ANC by the South African Communist Party, broke away to form the Pan Africanist Congress (PAC).   The PAC now largely inoperative was anti-Communist.   Led by Sobukwe, they engaged in a defiant campaign against the South African

Government. This led to clashes with the police and culminated in the clash at Sharpville on March 21, 1960.   It is estimated that 69 blacks were killed and 178 wounded. Sharpville was a turning point in South African history and resulted in the banning of both the ANC and PAC by the government in April 8, 1960.   As a result of these bannings, the ANC and the PAC went underground and formed military wings: the ANC formed Umkhonto We Sizwe (Spear of the Nation) and the PAC formed its military wing (POQO) [Pure].   These organizations commenced campaigns of sabotage and terrorism to achieve their ends.   While there is no evidence that POQO was ever infiltrated by Communists, Mr. Tambo stated in his speech to which I referred, that he welcomed the support and aid which the Communists so willingly offer.   He said, "We salute the SACP, particularly in the name of the combatants who have fallen in the course of our struggle as well as on behalf of the national leaders and militants presently held in the enemy's prisons."

The subcommittee heard testimony from Mr. Bartholomew Hlapane who stated that the sole source of funds for Umkhonto during the period that he acted as Treasurer of the South African Communist Party was the Communist Party.   Mr. Hlapane is a former member of the National Executive Committee of the ANC and served on these bodies during the years 1955–1964.   He testified that: "... no major decision could be taken by the ANC without the concurrence and approval of the Central Committee of the South African Communist Party.   Most major developments were in fact initiated by the Central Committee."   Mr. Hlapane further testified that:

> The Military Wing of the ANC, also known as Umkhonto We Sizwe, was the brainchild of the SACP, and, after the decision to create it had been taken, Joe Slovo and J.B. Marks were sent by the Central Committee of the SACP to Moscow to organize arms and ammunition and to raise funds for Umkhonto We Sizwe. (Joe Slovo, is now officially designated as "Deputy Chief" of

Umkhonto We Sizwe and is still a member of the National Executive Committee of the ANC and the Central Committee of the South African Communist Party.)

As far as the other witnesses from the ANC are concerned the Subcommittee concluded as follows:

To judge from the testimony of our younger ANC witnesses, little has changed. Mr. Ephraim Mfalapitsa received military and political training in Angola and the German Democratic Republic, likewise, Mr. Jeffrey Bosigo in Angola and the Soviet Union. Miss Nikonono Delphine Kave told a horrifying tale of indoctrination abuse and torture in Zambia, Botswana, and the USSR. Describing lectures in politics he received in Angola (at the Nova Catengue base where Cuban instructors, lecturers, and commanders supplemented those of Umkhonto We Sizwe), Mr. Bosigo has said, "... Every recruit was required to know the 'Freedom Charter' which was adopted by the African National Congress, the South African Congress of Trade Unions, and the South African Communist Party in 1955. We received lectures on Marx, Engels, Lenin, and Communist ideology. During all lectures the oppression of the black man in South Africa by the whites was emphasized, and we were told that we must fight for our freedom from the South African Government."

It should be noted that those witnesses who were former members of ANC and SWAPO exercised considerable courage in coming forward to testify, for it is the policy of those organizations to kill defectors. In fact, on December 16, 1982, less than two weeks after the publication of the Chairman's report, the ANC responded to the Chairman's offer to present its views. Mr. Bartholomew Hlapane was murdered, with his wife, Matilda, in their Soweto home by an ANC assassin using an AK-47 assault rifle. Their daughter Brenda, then 15, was paralyzed by the assassin's bullet. In 1983, an attempt was made on the life of Jeffery Bosigo, another ANC witness before the Subcommittee. However, Mr. Bosigo, recognizing he was at risk, had been authorized to carry a pistol. During the assissination attempt he shot and killed his assailant. He was subsequently tried and acquitted of all criminal charges.

Initially, MK acts of sabotage had been directed against what it termed the "Symbols of Apartheid," that is to say, it was content to blow up government buildings, electrical installations, and other facilities and in many of the trials which ensued, judges accepted the testimony in mitigation of the charges that efforts were made to preserve human life. That has now changed and in recent times members of MK have been guilty of indiscriminate killing of civilians, police officers, and whoever stands in their way.

Recently, three ANC members were convicted of high treason following attacks on a police station and were sentenced to death by the Supreme Court in Pretoria on June 8, 1982. Four policemen were killed and 10 others injured. The court heard testimony that a man who had his hands in the air was shot down in front of his wife. At 4:21 p.m. on Friday, May 20, 1983, Umkhonto We Sizwe struck again, detonating a bomb concealed in an automobile in a busy street in downtown Pretoria, South Africa's capital city, at a time when office workers were on their way home for the weekend. The blast killed 19 persons outright and injured 212. In a statement issued in *Dar Es Salaam* on May 23, the ANC proudly took credit for its act of terrorism, claiming that it constituted an attack on the South African military machine. What are the facts? Although some officers and administrative personnel of the South African Air Force have offices in one of the buildings damaged in the blast, and some of them were indeed among those killed and wounded, no fewer than 8 of the 19 persons killed and 54 of those seriously injured were black South Africans who were in the street, in a restaurant, and in a bank and other offices nearby. Two of the 19 dead were women, as were 71 of the injured. Three of the injured have suffered serious brain damage, at least one was blinded in both eyes, and another has lost a leg. People who are capable of planning such a heinous crime, let alone of executing it, have no claim whatsoever to speak for freedom or common decency.

From 1965 through December 15, 1983, the ANC has killed 56 people and wounded hundreds. This is the record of the development and evolution of the ANC into its present form. But what then of SWAPO? Is it also merely a pawn of the Soviet Union or does it exercise independence in a manner unlike the ANC?

SWAPO

The South West Africa People's Organization originally evolved from the Ovambo People's Congress which was formed at Cape Town by Ovambo workers in 1958. Among its most important founding members were Herman Toivo ja Toivo, Andreas Shipanga, Solomon Mifinawe, Emil Appolus, and Jariretundo Kozonguizi. Messers Shipanga and Kozonguizi both testified at the hearings. At the outset the organization already had contacts with the South African Liberal Party, the Congress of Democrats, the Wu Chi Chen (Chinese Guerrilla Warfare) and the African National Congress.

At the instigation of Mburumba Kerina, Toivo formed the Ovambo People's Organization in 1959 and was joined at that time by Sam Nujoma and Kerina. They received assistance from the Communist Party in South Africa. As a result of objections against the ethnic connotation which was attached to the new organization, SWAPO was formed in 1960, as the South West Africa People's Organization, the broader name being intended to attract territory-wide base of support. However, the Ovambo structure of the party never effectively changed and the Herero elements, which broke from the Ovambo People's Organization in 1959 to form the South West African National Union, never returned. While the broader name may not have attracted territory-wide political base, it undoubtedly assisted the organization in later obtaining international recognition as the sole representative of all of the Namibian people.

In the early stages SWAPO developed a collegial rule with Toivo in charge in Africa, Kerina at the United Nations and Shipanga and Nujoma operating in subordinate but important roles. By 1962 the group which previously advocated nonviolence made a conscious decision to move 180 degrees away from that approach. The USSR, China, Algeria, Ghana, and Tanzania made training facilities available to the SWAPO guerrillas. Toivo, who took personal command of the guerrillas, was captured and sent to Robben Island. Kerina had Nujoma appointed as first president of SWAPO. The divisions however developed into splits. The internal branch of SWAPO was less radical while the external branch undertook the guerrilla activities. The internal branch drew its support from church members, workers, and intellectuals who sought radical social reform through a kind of liberation theology. Less sophisticated members proclaimed their loyalty to the party because they perceived it as anti-white and anti-status quo. It was nevertheless made up of at least three factions. The external SWAPO was no less factionalized. Both wings of SWAPO refused to participate in the Turnhalle Conference in Namibia.

The disunity and friction within the leadership of SWAPO continued to increase and in March 1976, many of the younger activist members under the leadership of Andreas Shipanga met in Southern Zambia and itemized a list of grievances against the Nujoma administration. Shipanga was rebuffed by Nujoma when he and his followers demanded a new party Congress which would decide SWAPO's future direction. Shipanga and a large number of adherents attempted a protest march on Nujoma's headquarters in Lusaka; however, Nujoma persuaded President Kaunda to keep the "dissidents" in prison and Shipanga remained at Borma prison two years without a trial.

Mr. Shipanga and 12 other SWAPO dissidents were eventually released by Tanzania in May 1978. The Subcommittee has been unable to develop any information about the fate of other dissidents arrested at the same time. In his testimony Mr. Shipanga stated that 2,000 SWAPO members were arrested in April 1976 in Zambia in addition to the 600 who were released in April 1977 and the 13 who were released in May 1978, among them Shipanga. He does not know what happened to the others, who he last heard had been taken to Angola.

In July 1976 SWAPO, which had not previously described itself as a Marxist-Leninst party but rather as a "popular party," issued its political program, stating that its purpose was "to unite all Namibian people, particularly the working class, the peasantry, and progressive intellectuals into a vanguard party capable of safeguarding national independence and the building of a classless non-exploitive society based on the ideals and principles of scientific socialism." Dr. Crocker's testimony on his aspect of SWAPO's orientation before the Subcommittee was amply supported by the SWAPO witnesses. He stated that the U.S. Government estimates that SWAPO received about 90 percent of its military support and 50 percent of its overall support from communist sources. Advocate Kozonguizi also drew the Subcommittee's attention to the scale of the Soviet bloc's commitment to SWAPO, pointing to the large quantities of weapons and military equipment made available in Angola. The younger witnesses, Mr. Namolo and Mr. Hashiko, both former SWAPO cadre, testified in detail of their terrorist training in Angola by Soviet instructors. They also described their indoctrination in the USSR in "socialism and communism," "Leninist teachings," and "political economy."

Documents submitted for the record contain overwhelming evidence of the training of large number of SWAPO cadres in the USSR, both in military disciplines and, without exception, in Marxist-Leninist ideology. The position of "political commisar" is entrenched at all organizational levels of SWAPO. These men, selected on the basis of their educational attainments and understanding of ideology, are trained at the Komsonol Party School in the USSR, in the GDR, and in Cuba. Documents confirming this have been included in the record. On the basis both of the testimony presented and the documents obtained by the Subcommittee, the conclusion is is inescapable that the Soviets and their Communist allies within SWAPO insist that Marxist–Leninist doctrine is systematically taught to all who are recruited, or pressed into service in SWAPO or its military wing PLAN.

The U.N. recognizes SWAPO as the only representative of the Namibians and as a result of the special status, SWAPO received in 1981, 28 million dollars in food, education, medical, and vocational training projects. The U.N. Industries Development Organization (UNIDO) recently requested an additional 17.6 million dollars for an industrial management training program for Namibia. This would almost certainly be dominated by SWAPO. An additional source of U.N. backing for SWAPO is the UN High Commissioner for Refugees (UNHCR). From 1979 to 1981 it allocated about 10 million dollars for Namibian refugee camps--principally in Angola, SWAPO's main staging location for terrorist operations into Namibia. Moreover, the World Food Program (WFP) has given SWAPO 5.4 million dollars in food since 1974. The current WFP food gift budget for SWAPO is 2.8 million dollars. With the food provided, SWAPO is able to feed Namibian refugees in Angola, thereby using U.N. resources to sway the refugee population politically, and garner recruits for its military arm. Raids on SWAPO guerrilla camps in Angola disclosed a large volume of food cartons from the WFP which clearly were used to support the guerrilla forces.

It should be noted that during the hearings, evidence was developed that on August 8, 1977, Sam Nujoma, SWAPO President issued an order from U.N. Headquarters in New York to the SWAPO office in Luanda, Angola, for the assassination of political figures in northern Namibia. Two of the group were murdered. One of the men assassinated was the Paramount Chief of the Hereros, Clemens Kapuuo. Advocate Kozonguizi testified of the gruesome effect of SWAPO terrorism on the civilian population in northern Namibia. On the basis of their own experiences, both Mr. Namolo and Mr. Hashiko have testified about incidents such as the execution of a headman and the abduction by force of high school students by SWAPO cadres. Documents made available to the Subcommittee and included in the record confirm that such incidents are routine. In 1981, for example, 64 Namibian civilians were killed and 150 more were injured in explosions following the detonation of land mines by SWAPO forces. PLAN cadres, SWAPO's military wing, killed 94 civilians, including 11 local chiefs, a member of the Ovambo legislative assembly, and 4 deputy chiefs. Four chiefs, their wives, and a school principal were abducted and 58 incidents of sabotage involving damage to telephone lines, pipelines, bridges, and water ditches were reported. In 1983 through May 20th, 45 civilians were murdered and 187 were kidnapped from homes and schools. Scores of civilians were seriously injured in land mine incidents. Most of these victims are black.

Senator Denton concluded the hearings with the following comment:

> At the end of our hearings on the involvement of the Soviet Union and its surrogates in terrorism in southern Africa, we should review the testimony presented to the Subcommittee to extract and highlight the most important points.
>
> The hearings have elicited testimony which is at once shocking and familiar. It is familiar to those of us who have experience of the attempts, all too often successful, of Moscow and its agents to infiltrate and manipulate the so-called "national liberation movements" in Southeast Asia, Latin America, and Africa. It is surely shocking to all who prize liberty, democratic values, and human rights.
>
> As my distinguished colleague, Senator Pat Moynihan of New York, has remarked, the Communists have succeeded in appropriating the language of liberty. They cloak totalitarianism in the rhetoric of democracy. They conceal their expansionist goals with praiseworthy labels like "liberation" and "freedom." Who in our society would not identify with a "struggle for freedom"? The true irony is that the Soviets, whose tyranny over their own citizens has been so graphically

documented by writers like Aleksandr
Solzhenitsyn, and whose brutality towards those in
other societies who seek freedom was demonstrated in Hungary in 1956, in Czechoslovakia in
1968, in Afghanistan in 1979, and in Poland in
1981, nonetheless are allowed to represent themselves as the bearers of the flag of freedom in the
developing world."

I shall conclude with a quotation from Dr. Henry
Kissinger taken from a speech which he delivered in
Washington, D.C., during 1980, after the fall of the Shah of
Iran. I believe it to be appropriate to this subject.

It is true that American foreign policy must be
grounded in the humane values of our people and of
our democratic traditions. We would neither be
effective nor faithful to ourselves if we sought to
defend every status quo in an age of upheavals ...
[but] ... Iran should teach us that humane values
are not necessarily served by the overthrow of
conservative regimes. If we encourage upheavals
without putting in their place a moderate democratic alternative, a foreign policy conducted in
the name of justice and human rights, could wind
up by making the world safe for anti-American
radicalism.

PART FIVE
WESTERN EXPERIENCE

CHAPTER X

European Terrorism

Professor J. Sundberg

THE AREA

It is difficult without going into great detail to give anything more than an overview of what the European terrorism problem is all about. Let us start, however, with the area. What is Europe? However you want to measure it, it is something very big. It has about 380 million people west of the Socialist bloc. It has 21 countries belonging to the Council of Europe. It is an old battlefield that is replete with conflicts. It is also a very urbanized area. It houses much so-called "public opinion." Sometimes one may even wonder if the term "public opinion" does not simply mean the opinion held in Europe plus what people think in the United States.

In this area you will find a number of countries that are interesting from the point of view of terrorism. I will not touch France, but only events in Germany, Italy, and the Scandinavian area--particularly Sweden. All these countries have considerable experience in terrorism. Germany and Italy have hit the headlines in this matter for many years. Sweden is rather more the "green haven." With its recent peaceful, non-violent tradition it is an excellent resting place for terrorists when planning and regrouping.

THE SOCIALIST IDEOLOGY

The Marxist concept of law is of the universal kind. It claims to be valid for all people everywhere--even in the United States and Israel. Marxism includes a total concept of law and state: that means all law, inclusive international law, and all states, inclusive of the United States and Sweden. The Marxist message runs as follows, as it has been put together on the basis of a number of classical Soviet manuals:[1]

> Every people and every nation have a right to self-determination. Self-determination consists of a people or a nation throwing off the imperial control of the bourgeois class. A people or nation that has thus exercised its right of self-determination is then independent and equal with all other people. When equal independent peoples or nations form a state, popular and national sovereignty merge with state sovereignty, and any subsequent attempt to induce a change in the social system or government in that state is an infringement of state sovereignty. However, any people or nation that has not exercised such self-determination [that is, throwing off the control of the bourgeois class imperialists] still has the right to do so, and any subsequent attempt to induce a change of the social system or government in that state is not an infringement of the sovereignty of that state.

This is an excellent message in a way. It is just as good as a religious explanation: "God is with us," because it means that history is a one-way street. It can only end with the workers and labor masses becoming the ruling class. Any other turn of history is a perversion. Such a perversion has to be countered with all force, including armed force. If you look at this message in the terms of detente which is the period I am going to cover, it means that countries must live in peace and cooperate even if their social systems are different. However, the principle of peaceful coexistence does not apply to relations between oppressor and oppressed, between the colonialists and the victims of colonialist oppression. The essence of the contradiction is thus this uncompromising ideological struggle in which only one limit applies, and that is that international peace should not be undermined. Unless the capitalists give in, overthrowing them is a revolutionary process done by organized armed violence. Summarizing the message, it means a belief in the predetermined advance of civilization and the acceptance of an overriding legal duty to prepare for and assist in this overthrowing, whenever necessary by armed force. Once a duty to further advance civilization is accepted--if necessary, by armed force--important consequences follow because, beside the states, the revolutionary movements are entitled to further such advances. So they have a right to engage in wars of liberation--wars that are intended to liberate people from capitalist slavery or to liberate colonies and dependent countries from the yoke of imperialism. As a consequence, of this right to resort to revolutionary war by the nationalists which these movements are considered to represent have been accepted as international law subjects.

To summarize in practical Western, non-Socialist terms, this means that the government is always wrong and that the bourgeois class is always wrong. From a moral-legal point of view it is universally fail-safe. Any revolutionary group is always right. It is all only a question of the right implementation of the basic Marxist message.

THE KOREAN WAR AND ITS AFTERMATH

The Korean War, from a Socialist point of view, was a lost war. The workers did not rise. The Communist regime did not stay. In fact, the war ended with an armistice which put the border at about the same place where the war started. So it was a severe rebuff for the Communist bloc. It was unprecedented. It had not happened before.

The unexpected result of the Korean War meant that some soul-searching took place in Moscow. Moscow had to find out what went wrong and why the war ended so badly. There was a drawn-out discussion, fully open as I understand it. The result was the conclusion that it had been wrong to concentrate on the workers and the peasants. So something else should be tried; it was decided to focus on the intelligentsia. They did so, and the next war--the Vietnam War--was not a lost war from a Socialist point of view.

THE TRI-CONTINENTAL CONGRESS

The triggering event for the new line would seem to be the Tri-Continental Congress in Havana in 1966. In those days it was not much noticed in Europe, but it came to influence, or at least be reflected, in subsequent events. One of the results of the Congress was the setting up of a permanent organization (OSPAAL) and a magazine, the *Tricontinental*. In one of the early numbers of this magazine Carlos Marighella's *Minimanual for the Urban Guerrilla* was reprinted. The Tri-Continental Congress added prestige and consistency to the revolutionary fight in Latin America. It gave some guidance to revolutionary movements and some extra respectability to them since they were now seen as being represented by the bloc behind the Tri-Continental. The Congress also meant the giving up of the idea of the rural war and turning to the urban guerrilla war: everything that was difficult for the rural guerrilla was easy for the urban guerrilla. One of the more remarkable events in the wake of the Tri-Continental Congress was the rise of the Tupamaros in Uruguay. When the Uruguayan economy went into a tailspin, there followed a military take-over and in opposition thereto the Tupamaros came into being. It carried on an intelligentsia type of struggle, implementing the Tri-Continental Congress principles, and was widely publicized in Europe. The Tupamaros enjoyed a very sympathetic press and exerted a considerable radiation into Europe. It had glamour. Many European youth felt that these young students were doing

the type of thing that any intelligent young student should
do.

LATIN AMERICAN RADIATION: GERMANY

Europe is an extremely urbanized area, placed in the
vicinity of a superpower that was immediately identified
with the basic philosophical message previously referred to.
Even if some might say that the philosophical message was
misinterpreted, the identity was still there. It was like
Christianity: there are all sorts of variations of the
Christian message but one can still discover an essential
area which remains the same and which makes the believers
Christian rather than Moslem or Mosaic.

One may say that in Europe modern terrorism started in
Germany; and in Germany it started in Berlin. Berlin was
and still is a divided city full of drama. Part of the problem
was that West Berlin was full of young intellectuals without
a history, because post-war Germany is characterized by its
absence of history. German history being suppressed by
the victors of the Second World War, the young had no
chance of knowing it. That lack made for an absence of
perspective among the young Germans in the very German
perception of the world. Furthermore, Berlin was a city
replete with draft dodgers. It was a demilitarized area
where no military service was required. So everybody who
did not like military service for various reasons--and there
are many--undertook studies in Berlin. In this environment things started to happen. There were various
incidents and anti-establishment organizations started to
appear.

The Baader-Mienhof group was made up of a clever
woman and a smart young man. The woman was editing a
newspaper financed by socialist sympathizers. After a
while her interpretation of the socialist message became
"Destroy! You have to destroy society in order to make
room for a rebirth." Her basic message may perhaps be
condensed into the phrase, "It is better to burn a
department store than to run one." Indeed, she put fire to
a department store. Certainly this was a crucial event.

The Baader-Meinhof group's interpretation was that they needed publicity in order to wake up the workers.   The only means to publicity that would be effective would be by throwing bombs.   Indeed, it was very effective.   But once bomb-throwing started, the gang became involved in a fight with the law enforcement forces.   One of the things that was remarkable was the considerable public support that Baader-Meinhof enjoyed.   Group members, when not on the run but relaxing somewhere, wrote letters to leading leftists ("liberals"), asking for donations, and donations came in considerable amounts.   Financing seems to have been rather easy: they had the donations, they had what they collected from bank robberies, and finally they collected from theatrical kidnappings.

From the Baader-Meinhof point of view, their campaign ended badly.   The group members were eventually caught and placed in the Stammheim Prison awaiting what became a mammoth trial, done with perfect German competence, diligence, and patience.   But then an extremely remarkable thing happened.   From their prison cells in Stammheim the group members ran the whole terrorist underground movement in Germany.   Their radiation was so charismatic that they could discipline the underground forces by simply saying: "If you do not obey, we will deny you."   This was a sufficient rebuff to discipline the man or the woman and to make him or her comply.   So from their prison cells they exercised complete discipline in the movement.   Commands were given by certain technical methods with a lawyer's office in Stuttgart playing a significant role.   Through this lawyer's office the group was organizing, indeed creating, the other side of the terrorist movement.

A terrorist movement--I am using the term loosely-- has two branches.   One branch includes the people who do the daring things: throwing the bombs and sometimes getting killed, engaging in shootouts with the police, putting up posters, and participating in aggressive activities.   The other branch is the major organization.   It consists of the sympathizers, those who send money, provide shelter and transportation, and provide publicity.   Because there have been a few turncoats in the Baader-Meinhof environment, we know a great deal about how the operation was run. By these means the Baader-Meinhof group succeeded in establishing cells--support committees--all over the world. They succeeded in attracting publicity, giving interviews, appearing on television shows, and working congenially with the media. All this did not help the group members because they all ended their lives in the Stammheim Prison. But it certainly had a tremendous impact on the general thinking and this impact is the lasting achievement of the Baader-Meinhof gang. A side effect of that impact is the group's surprising ability to recreate its movement in new generations.

Let me try to summarize the achievements of the Baader-Meinhof group. First, they broke up the German consensus. I think it is right to attribute the falling apart of German political thinking to that movement. It was a catalyzing event. Second, they succeeded in creating the theme in which the socialist revolutionary goals were phrased, and how the headlines were phrased to influence the general thinking. Lastly, the members of the group immortalized themselves. They were active only a short time and in a limited area but their names became known the world over. Their impact on world history will have to be assessed on the basis of future facts not yet known but what we know so far allows the conclusion that their importance cannot be judged only from the time they spent and the area they traversed.

THE RADIATION SPREADS: SWEDEN

The success of the Baader-Meinhof movement showed itself in some of the after-generations. One among these after-generations was the *Socialist Patients Collective*. It was the creation of Dr. Wolfgang Huber and his wife Ursula at the Psychiatric Neurological Clinic of Heidelberg University. Dr. Huber was a good psychiatrist of some standing. He organized his patients into a group that felt that by blowing up society, or pieces of it such as police barracks, government offices, and other facilities could relieve themselves of their illness, that is, by destroying

society you made yourself healthy.   This is the group from
which most of the people came who captured the Federal
German Embassy in Stockholm.   They were the ones who
went in, assaulted the Embassy, took it over, took the
ambassador prisoner, killed off the military attache, and
finally blew up the whole place.

One might think that this was purely the work of
maniacs.   However, in a way the event is symptomatic,
because it is the socialist message introduced into the
closed world of socialist mental patients that performs the
trick.   Blowing up the West German Embassy was a feat
that made headlines all over the world.   Indeed it had an
effect in Sweden.   The whole drama was well televised
and it was a great drama.   One of those watching was a
German who claimed to have belonged to the Second June
Movement (another organization in the German terrorist
underground), although perhaps it was no more than
bragging.   He was on the run and had taken refuge in
Sweden which is the "green haven" in these connections.
Sweden is that country where the people in the movements
relax, build up resources, and do their planning before they
move out into the real battlefield on the rest of the
Continent.   A German, Norbert Kroecher, watched   the
attack on the West German Embassy, but he was not
pleased.   He was not pleased it seems because he was not
privy to the plan that he saw being implemented while
watching television.   This is an inference from what was
revealed at the subsequent trials with the Kroecher group.
Kroecher felt that he had been left out as unimportant by
his fellows in the terrorist field.   So he decided to outdo
them, to show them that he was a better terrorist than they
were.   This feeling made him start conceiving his plans,
which included the taking of the former Swedish Minister of
the Interior as a hostage.   The purpose was to extort the
consent of the Swedish Government to exercise pressure on
the German Government to release the Baader-Meinhof
people.   It was a simple plan, perfectly rational within the
framework of his thinking.   But it did not work.

ITALY

A feature of the Communist Party is its insistence on discipline but not everybody is in favor of strict discipline, certainly not on the far left.   As a result a great number of splinter groups are continuously forming and some of these groups sometimes get to be well organized.   In the 1970s a number of terrorist groups emerged.   From a tactical point of view one could say that they belonged to either of two major groupings: the Brigate Rossi on the one side, and on the other side something that sometimes is called the Autonomous Collectives.   What is very characteristic of the Italian scene is the cultivation of the second force that is necessary for a terrorist activity to be successful, i.e., the sympathizers.   In that area the Italian terrorists were extremely successful and that may have been their main achievement because it seems that at present the terrorist tide is declining only due to the successes of the Italian police.   However, this is a dangerous area for speculation.

SWEDEN

The Scandinavian countries form an area close to the German scene and one to which Germans often go.   Lately this area has had a very peaceful tradition.   It has few conflicts and if there are conflicts they are normally not important.   Postwar migrations, however, made the Swedes import some foreign ideological.   Among the immigrants were the Croats who brought their own quarrels with the Serbs and others with them.   In a similar way the Chileans brought along many ideas about how to change things in Chile.   Indeed, a great deal of immigrants coming from all over the world settled in Sweden.[2]   Most immigrants are of course basically peaceful.   What emerged in the course of the Kroecher inquiry, however, was that the Scandinavian area offered access to the sympathizers and it has been possible to find sufficient sympathizers in Sweden to set up organizations of sympathizers.   One such organization upon which the success of the Baader-Meinhof group depended, was the "Committees against the Isolation

Torture" which was discretely run from the Stammheim Prison cells.

Sweden was important to the German terrorist scene. Some of its financing came from Sweden. When some of the books and pamphlets were placed under censorship so that they could not be printed in Germany, they were printed in Sweden instead.[3] Kroecher, who came to Sweden as a refugee on the run from German justice and could not speak a word of Swedish, still succeeded in existing in Sweden for five years at the expense of a Swedish girlfirend belonging to the sympathizers. In this Swedish environment Kroecher succeeded in recruiting a fully capable group that could have carried through his plan against the former Minister of the Interior had Kroecher not run out of luck. The group included a 'killer.' Killers could be recruited from among the Latin American revolutionaries who could be spotted at various places such as the Stockholm Refugee Council. The Kroecher group recruited a man who had received his training in North Korea, likewise some Chileans were also recruited. Together these foreigners formed a nucleus in the Kroecher group and the killer was its 'policeman.' This made the enforcement of discipline possible in spite of the rather loose composition of the group. The concept of the "green haven" was no bar.

Currently, in the "green haven" of Sweden there is not much terrorism to be seen--things rarely go up in flames, there are no bombs thrown around. But it is an area for reorganization and for planning. It is an area where the Iranians and the Turks come to rest. There is no doubt in my mind that they are contributing to the Socialist revolutionary cause.

NOTES

1.   Dorsey, *Towards World Perspectives of Philosophy of Law and Social Philosophy, Contemporary Conceptions of Law*. Paper contributed to World Congress of Philosophy of Law and Social Philosophy, (Basel 1979), p 28.

2.   J. Sundberg, The Antiterrorist Legislation in Sweden, in
Crelinsten, Laberge-Altmejd and Szaboede.   Terrorism and
Criminal Justice (Lexington, Books 1979), 71 ff.
3.   See e.g., the volume: "texte: der RAF," Verlag Bo
Cavefors.   Malmo.

CHAPTER XI

French Democracy versus Terrorism: Attitudes, Policy, Laws, and the Press

Professor C. Franck

"French democracy versus terrorism" is a subject which is almost untreatable. "Versus" is not the word which applies, in any sense, to the attitudes of the successive French governments towards terrorism and this is true also for many French newspapers and French television.

First, France is in a very particular situation concerning the terrorist problem because she suffers and has been suffering for many years of terrorism. For instance, in the last two years, 27 civilians have been killed and more than 200 wounded. But the unique characteristic is that this terrorism is not indigenous. Of course this makes terrorism in France significantly different from the situation in Germany with the Baader-Meinhof gang, in Italy with the Red Brigade, and all the rest, and even the situation in Great Britain with the IRA. The thrust is that all the attempts to set up a genuine, really French, terrorist movement have completely failed during those years. The only one which tried to exist, the so-called "Action Directe Gang," never had more than 10 members at a time. The problem is really one of dealing with traveling terrorists who, from time to time, operate within the limits of French territory. France is nevertheless a laboratory for the approach of the terrorist problem.

I think that three points are extremely important because they illustrate some of the theoretical discoveries which have been made by other reporters of terrorist actions.

First, France is an illustration of the difficulty in drawing a line between terrorists and freedom fighters. Second, it is also a living example of the distortion of semantics by some of the media, usually, and--this is very important--infiltrated by devout friends or agents of terrorists. Third, the attitudes and the behavior of the politicians and journalists to terrorism is neither perceived nor understood as a problem of definition, but as a problem of legitimacy.

Difficulties arise in drawing a line extending from the fact that there is no legal definition of terrorism in French law. For instance, as far as incrimination is concerned, this concept is totally unknown to French criminal law. Some readers who may be more familiar with French law might be surprised that a country with such experience in extraordinary criminal court proceedings ignores the labelling of a terrorist act or the definition of a terrorist act. One must remember that those extraordinary courts were set up by successive governments after World War II, especially by General de Gaulle, to deal with those people who were regarded as enemies of the state and, in the case of de Gaulle, to deal with his former friends whose help he needed in 1958 to regain power. Therefore, the jurisdiction of those courts was not based on terrorist acts. It was based on the intentions of the offender to overthrow the government by violence. It is clear that it may in some cases have a link with acts of terrorism; but the acts of terrorism are, of course, a much larger concept because most of the acts of terrorism in recent years were not aimed at overthrowing the government but at killing people who did not have anything to do with the French Government or the French state.

Second, is the distortion by some of the media of the meaning of terrorism and resistance. The most important

roles in regard to this distortion are played by the
newspapers and television. Television is a state monopoly
in France, it always was and still is under tight control of
the government and it must serve the propaganda purposes
of the government. Journalists who serve on the three
state-run television networks may be fired overnight, so
they must do what the government asks them to do. Their
dependence helps the government in the distortion of the
truth and the distortion of what is terrorism and what is a
national liberation movement. To understand what the
television says one must bear in mind the fact of the French
Government's position concerning most of the terrorist
acts. The government believes that by giving into at least
some of the terrorists political demands the terrorists will
be softened, appeased, and they will come to behave like
normal human beings. They will no longer have any reason
to behave and act like terrorists.

This is particularly true of the approach to the PLO
terrorist group. The big lie or hoax that television has
been spreading for years is that the PLO has recognized
Israel "by implication." In the French language the words
have a worse effect than in English. In English the words
"by implication' have a very restrictive meaning which is
not the same as the French "implicite." Therefore, the
average Frenchman has been misled into believing that the
PLO has recognized Israel once and for all. The problem
with spreading this lie is that from time to time the top
leadership of the PLO denies it. Sometimes these denials
are displayed on the screen as a direct scoop when the
government does not have a chance to avoid it.

For instance, on January 24, 1983, Yasser Arafat was
interviewed by the French television "Antenne 2." This
was three or four months after the Fes summit conference,
which was celebrated as "the recognition by implication" of
Israel by the PLO. The first question asked by the
journalist named Serra was, "Do you recognize by
implication the state of Israel?" Arafat laughed for five
minutes. Then the journalist got impatient and said, "I
flew to Tunis only to interview you and you don't give me an
answer." Then the answer was, "The recognition? What

kind of recognition? We are the only owners of the country; they are the occupiers. They are the killers and we are the victims." And that was the end of the interview.

There is another example. In December, 1982, the PLO blew up a civilian bus in Jerusalem, killing six people. Responsibility for this act of indiscriminate terror was claimed by the PLO immediately. The next day, a French journalist (who is Jewish) commented on the television, "Mr Arafat is now blockaded in Tripoli by the Syrians. So he couldn't confirm or deny his responsibility." This is the kind of lie you hear almost every day on the various French television networks. Of course, no denial is possible as one has no access to the television. But the purpose of this lie must be made clear. It is the trick by which the French Government has been trying to convince the population that the PLO uses violence because they are compelled by the Israeli stubbornness in refusing to acknowledge the rights of the Palestinians, while the PLO recognizes the existence of Israel as a state.

The pattern of lies that are involved was invented years ago by an Egyptian Jew, whose name is Elie Raffoul and who has been writing and still writes under a pen name --Eric Rouleau. Rouleau invented that story more than 10 years ago. Then it was adopted by television on government instructions to support its false policy. Rouleau is one of the founders of the Egyptian communist party in Egypt, along with Curiel, the most formidable terrorist of the century. When all Jews, including his father and his brother, were expelled from Egypt by Nasser, Rouleau started a brilliant career as a civil servant in the Propaganda Ministry of Egypt run by Hassanen Heykal, who was the official theorist of Nasserism.

Rouleau came to France in the early 1960's and managed to become the specialist on the Near and Middle East affairs of the widespread daily paper, *Le Monde*. First he tried this lie, "recognition by implication" of Israel by Nasser after the Six Day War. When Nasser died, he tried the same line for the PLO and managed to reverse the roles and to reverse the truth. Then he began to insult

Sadat, who was about to make peace with Israel and who had some convincing means of pressure on *Le Monde*. It is not hard to imagine what type of means he had since Rouleau was ousted from his job as the man in charge of the Near and Middle East Department. Rouleau took a one year leave in the USA; but before he left, he wrote a book in collaboration with Mr Abou Iyad, Number 2 man in the PLO. This book, entitled *Palestinian Sans Patria (Palestinian Without a Fatherland)* in which he claimed that the PLO would never recognize the state of Israel and that the PLO state in Samaria, Judea, and Gaza is the first step in the physical destruction of the state of Israel. It was proven to be the very opposite that the same Mr Rouleau was writing in *Le Monde* a few weeks before. Later he was, inter alia, special correspondent to Teheran, where Khomeini had invited him. After Sadat's death, he was immediately restored to his former position in *Le Monde*.

Why devote so much time to this topic? Because *Le Monde* in France carries great influence and is the only French paper which has a serious reputation. The standards of French papers are not high. *Le Monde*, with long articles covering almost every subject, seems to be a serious paper. Moreover, it claims to be neutral and impartial. Actually, it is a very militant paper, and Rouleau's hatred of Israel is shared by its staff. For instance, Andre Fontaine, the greatest authority on foreign policy in *Le Monde* has also been spreading the lie that the PLO accepts Israel by implication. If the PLO accepts Israel, the argument runs, it is up to Israel to make concessions. If Israel does not make concessions, the PLO has a right to fight. Therefore, the PLO people are never terrorists, but freedom fighters. The confluence of *Le Monde* and of the television networks has made it an acceptable truth. Today the PLO is a national liberation movement fighting only for a state in Judea, Samaria, and Gaza. Moreover, it is in the interest of Israel to accept this logic, because then Israel would be at peace. Therefore, there is no reason for Israel not to do so, except that Israel has an imperialistic view and it wants to expand at the expense of the poor Palestinian people.

Today, such is the extended view of the press. I had another occasion to recently realize it through a personal encounter in July 1983, with another paper not as influential as *Le Monde*, but, *Le Matin de Paris*, which is the unofficial Socialist paper. Many years ago Mr Begin appointed me to be a translator and be responsible for the French edition of *The Revolt*. I was warned by the publisher at the time that advertisements about excerpts from *The Revolt* were appearing in *Le Matin de Paris*. They made notices in two column widths with one column containing a CID photo of Begin which had been distributed between 1944 and 1948, and in the other the mention that before becoming the Prime Minister of Israel Mr Begin was a very feared terrorist. This notice appeared five or six days in succession in *Le Matin de Paris*. I had a right to threaten legal action because such excerpts cannot be reproduced without permission and I compelled them to stop the advertisement. On that occasion I had a long discussion with the chief editor and his deputy and I instructed them in the difference between terrorism and resistance. They would not believe me for the simple reason the problem is not one of definition, but of legitimacy. Today the propaganda action of the television networks and most of the newspapers, headed by *Le Monde*, has such an impact that most people believe that the legitimacy is on the side of the PLO. Therefore, whatever the PLO does is moral and done for the Palestinians who want peace with Israel. On the other hand, the press describes Israeli actions in pejorative terms. The refusal of Israel to acknowledge that so-called "recognition by implication" is explained by the fact that Israel wants a greater Israel, and it wants to occupy territories which are not Israeli. The two words you very often hear coupled in the French media are "greater Israel" and "occupied territories." The connotation of the "greater Israel" in France is an emotional one because greater Israel reminds the French of greater Germany, notwithstanding the fact that greater Israel is smaller than Belgium. But people don't know that. The connotation of occupied territory is even more damaging because this is exactly the word used for the definition of the four years of

1940-1944 during which France was occupied by Germany. The period is known in the history of France as the Occupation. One can imagine the atmosphere that has been created. It legitimizes everything the terrorists do, especially the PLO underground fighting to free occupied territories.

Today the French Government has succeeded in making the population consent to a policy of appeasement towards terrorist groups by giving in to their plans. It is not only true with the PLO but with the Armenians, since President Mitterrand said that Turkey should admit to the 1915 massacre of Armenians. He added, of course, that this massacre doesn't excuse those who commit crimes in France against civilians who have nothing to do with Turkey. But the Armenians have claims.... The French conclude that they are justifiable. It is also true about the Basque Nationalist movement (ETA) which has had strong French support for many years. Only recently this support has weakened because the Socialist Government in Spain has exerted strong pressure for more than a year on fellow socialist Mitterrand, who at last gave in. For the first time since Spain returned to democracy in 1977, France has acted against the ETA, which previously had been given a free hand to operate from France.

In conclusion, the irony of the official French position toward terrorism was disclosed recently by the satirical weekly *Le Canard Enchaine*, and soon followed by the rest of the press, that the Undersecretary of State for Public Security in the French Government, Mr Franceschi, has had two or more meetings at his private residence with Abou Iyad, Number Two man in the PLO, in order to protect the French people against terrorism.

PART SIX
FUTURE PERSPECTIVES

CHAPTER XII

Unconventional Terrism—A Glance into the Future

Professor Y. Dror

Permit me to draw a pointilistic picture of terrorism in the form of nine observations which, may add up not to a comprehensive, in-depth analysis, but to a reconnaissance or an exploration of some relevant issues related to the open-ended, uncertainty-shrouded subject of the future of unconventional terrorism.

Point number one is a warning to writers like myself. It is enough that we have unconventional terrorists: we do not want to have any crazy analysts, that is, writers on the subject who give good ideas to be misused by others. Therefore, I must restrain the temptation to provide some very picturesque scenarios of what unconventional terrorism might and can do because I would not like something like this to happen next year. Therefore, this is a subject that should be handled in a sanitized way. It is better to be less attractive to the mass media than to provide too good ideas to bad guys, as sometimes happens.

The second point revolves around the key question which really has no answer, which is not "Will conventional terrorism occur?", which we don't know; rather, the real key question is "Why doesn't unconventional terrorism happen now?". The technology and the knowledge are around, and some terrorists groups have it. Unconventional does not mean nuclear. Nuclear terrorism is a completely different matter. But, there is no problem for present terrorist groups to escalate terrorism significantly. Why does it not happen? We do not know. Probably the answer is not that the use of escalated methods would not realize their goals, because many terrorist groups use means which do not advance their declared goals. I think the answer is more that terrorist groups are not always more innovative than governments. In other words, they tend to become frozen in certain tactics. There was a wave of innovation and there are a number of terrorist entrepeneurs who invented or reinvented new forms of conflict. These inventions were disseminated to others. A new wave of different forms may come if and when such terrorism entrepeneurs arise and the conditions encourage spread. True, terrorism deviates from certain accepted rules. But it also has become stylized, and the stylization of terrorism helps its handling and absorption. I think the lack of inventiveness shared by all organizations explains in part why terrorism has not yet escalated. There may also be factors of cost-benefit analysis on their part, but I would not rely on simple rationalistic explanations. The fact that no reliable answer can be provided to the question, "Why isn't terrorism escalating more than it has, even though such escalation is technologically feasible?", leads to the question, "Will terrorism escalate?". I think the answer will have to take the following form: (a) it is feasible; (b) which means it may happen; (c) there is no basis for allocating probabilities to its occurrence in a specific form and location.

The patterns of terrorism are not regular enough to permit prediction by extrapolation. The relevant social and psychological dynamics are not known well enough to permit process prediction. We are in a field of uncertainty. But, as escalated terrorism is possible, and may come, the decision principle of "minimum regret" forces us to prepare for it. The principle of "minimum regret" asks under which error do we pay less:

Error 1.   We do not prepare and it happens.
Error 2.   We prepare and it does not happen.
It takes a large amount of preparation, at least in staff work and readying of suitable instruments, to take rapid action if and when unconventional terrorism materializes. The error of preparing and it does not come is superior to not being prepared and it does come.   Therefore, I think that a reasonable analysis of the issue leads to the conclusion that significant preparation should be undertaken in the face of uncertainty, to face the possible occurrence of unconventional terrorism.   But, investments in such preparations, including preventive measures, should not be too expensive.   I am using qualitative terms.   But this argument can be operationalized and I will provide some indications, starting with point number three.

To penetrate deeper into the matter, some daring conjectures, even if they cannot be supported fully, on the causes of jumps in terrorism have to be made.   Let me just provide a number of such daring propositions.   I cannot prove them, but they are supported by historic material as reasonable conjectures.   I will illustrate the approach by identifying a number of social characteristics which might contribute to terrorism.

- One can look at terrorism as an epidemic.   An epidemic, a term taken from medicine, is a disease which breaks out from time to time violently, but its causes and sources are endemic.   I think terrorism is endemic to rapid social change.   The world is in an open-ended process of transformations in values, technology, and global structure.   One of the side effects of such change is a loosening of accepted ways of doing things.   Relaxation may find as one of its expressions deviate behavior in the statistical sense, and also in the moral sense.   These processes may, among other things, be expected to take the form of various forms of terrorism.
- I've been doing quite a bit of reading on the psychology of saints.   Then I asked myself the following question: In modern Western society,

what can people who would have become saints in
earlier periods do?   What would people who in other
societies become adventurers do?   It may well be
that modern societies do not provide career patterns
in the legitimate order for certain types of
personalities who may, instead, move into extra-
legal activities such as terrorism.   So, some features
of modern society which do not provide fitting roles
for certain personality types, may structurally cause
terrorism.

● Historically, there are societies and cultures with a
kind of millenial culture. I have been reading some
German literature, analyzing Russia in those terms.
If there is anything to such types of hermeneutic,
historic speculations, it may help to discuss propen-
sities of different cultures to move into unconventional "Judgment Day"-oriented activities such as
escalating terrorism. For instance, what I have
elsewhere called crazy states, is a pure type
illustration of such behavior.

Point number four concerns the meaning of unconventional.   Having explored some dimensions of unconventional terrorism, it is time I specify that term.   The term
does not refer exclusively to weapons systems, and certainly
not to so-called nuclear devices.   Unconventional is a
relative term.   For sure, when the first cars appeared in
England they were an unconventional mode of transportation.   Now, horses have become an unconventional mode of
transportation.   In comparison to present terrorism, which
for better or worse we have become used to (or perhaps a
little immunized to) unconventional terrorism can take
quite different forms, of which I will mention three without
providing concrete scenarios.

1. Targets may change. For instance, terrorists may
   move against symbolic targets of value, monuments
   of society, with shattering effects.
2. There can be escalation in the usual sense in
   weapons systems, such as new types of explosives.

Biotoxical possibilities have also been discussed in the literature.

3. There may be escalation in tactics or strategy. For instance, overloading the defensive system by many simultaneous acts, or more sophisticated threat methods.

Such possibilities lead to intellectually interesting but horrifying possibilities of augmented terror psychological effects. A main way to look on some features of present terrorism, in addition to political and some security effects, is the effect of traumatic episodes on society. As long as dramatic experiences of terror are easily contained, and one gets used to them, something Israel has been relatively successful in, not much damage occurs. But if the psychological effects are augmented--and I could easily provide scenarios of minor acts which could completely terrorize, in the psychlogical sense of the term, large masses of the population by the effects of demonstrations-- societies can be thrown into a tantrum. Such psychological threats present one of the main difficulties facing governments: to gauge the public reaction to potential terrorist acts in order to judge whether or not to take such potential terrorist acts seriously and challenge a possible bluff.

In point number five we examine the responses to risks. The vulnerabilities of societies may increase with modern democratic societies disliking risks; they become more adverse to risk. If, indeed, Western societies show tendencies to have a reduced tolerance for risks, they may become very vulnerable to the psychlogical traumatization of dramatic terrorism, such as unconventional incidents accompanied by threats of more to come.

Point number six leads to a broader domain, namely, a comparison of the strengths and weaknesses of Western liberal democratic societies and totalitarian societies. I would say that in some sense, the totalitarian state is vulnerable. Such as in its sensitivity to a case of what one called here "the bullet"; the bullet hitting the central person on whom the totalitarian system is built. But totalitarian states make strenuous efforts to prevent terrorism, and they are very efficient at it. They arrest not only people that are terrorists, but people that might become terrorists. It can include millions, as happened in the Stalin regime or the Hitler regime. So, if you are looking for very efficient ways to fight terrorism, this would lead to totalitarian measures. But care must be taken not to let terrorism in this way undermine democracy. Let us take three dimensions only. One is the readiness to use terrorism as a weapon; the second is vulnerability; and the third is the ability to take strong countermeasures such as strict control of population movement, control over access to information, and other measures. In all these three dimensions, democracy is handicapped. Democracy is not ready to use terrorism and related tools as a weapon in international conflict. Democracies are, in some respect, more vulnerable; and democracies are less willing to use stricter countermeasures. For example, in the United States the idea of having the population carry identity papers is regarded as undemocratic.

We may run here into the unpleasant possibility, even if not with high probability, that if escalated forms of terrorism become a more important mode of conflict, the security handicaps of democracies could threaten their survival. This is a subset of the broader question of the relative advantages and disadvantages of democracies, not as pleasant places to live in, which is not in debate, but in the tough competition for influencing the future culture of humanity in a period of social, political, and ideological transformations. The optimistic assumptions that the beautiful is sure to win in the end, regretfully has no historical support. One has to work for the beautiful, and terrorism is part of this problem.

Point number seven asks, "Can unconventional terrorism be handled?" Handled does not mean totally prevented; handled means absorbed, reduced, and contained, in ways that no fundamental damage to the fabric of democracy ensues. I think it can. But it requires a number of innovations. I mention some in other writings. Let me here mention just a few.

We may have to pay small prices in liberal values to preserve the real essence of democracy, such as identity papers in countries that do not have them now. One may have to change some doctrines of international law, especially the doctrine of state liability in the sense of imposing responsibilities for terrorism on states. This involves the duties to refrain from active support of terrorism and to prevent preparations for escalated terrorism in their territory. In principle a doctrine of counteraction against countries that do engage in active support of terrorism are an essential innovation in international law of the free world.

I had the pleasure of participating in a conference on the legal aspect of terrorism in Washington, D.C. Entebbe was discussed. Most of the lawyers were ready to look for some exception to the doctrine of sovereignty in order to excuse Israel of an illegal act. But none of the lawyers there, other than myself, was ready to propose a positive doctrine stating that it is part of the legitimate right of self-defense of a country to take active action against terrorist activities, terrorist infrastructure, and terrorist safehouses in other countries, if the host country does not take the appropriate action on its own. I agree; this would increase anarchy in an orderly world. But in a partly chaotic world, it may help to reintroduce some sense of responsibility in countries which can support active terrorism without any risk to themselves. The delicate subject of Iran's taking U.S. hostages in Teheran provides another illustration. Would the Iranians ever have done it to the Soviet Union? In other words, a question must be raised: What visible--if not dramatic--penalities did Iran pay for this feat? Penalty must be exacted, not as "revenge" for this case, but in order to reduce the probability of it's happening somewhere else. These qustions must be faced in order to prepare ourselves for escalated terrorism.

Point number eight is that escalated terrorism should really be analyzed in terms of learning capacities. A main dimension of the capacity to govern in a changing world is the ability to learn. To simplify it, there are three levels of the capacity to learn:

1. Anticipatory learning--that we recognize possible events in the future and prepare ourselves.
2. Fast learning--we do not prepare ourselves in advance, but once an event happens we learn quickly and correctly.
3. Slow learning and mislearning--studies of governmental behaviour on a comparative and historic basis indicate that slow and incorrect learning has been common to governments and probably will continue.

If unconventional terrorism happens, and I don't say it will, but if and when it happens, how rapidly will governments adjust themselves without getting hysterical and overreacting? Governments need to improve their learning capacities in order to contain terrorism. Their education requires separate treatment.

Point number nine returns to the role of analysts and scholars. I started by saying that they should not make themselves famous or infamous by throwing out brilliant illustrations of possible horrible deeds. But they can do their share by trying to think ahead on such issues so that they are ready if and when unconventional terror strikes and politicians might be open to some innovations. Let us be ready for that by unconventional thinking.

Let me add that in the long run, democracies are less prone to terrorism than totalitarian states. But the "long run" is far off.

CHAPTER XIII

Summary: For Global War
to Terrorism

Professor Y. Ne'eman

War is terrible. With the evolution of humanism, it has become natural for most cultures to do the utmost to avoid it, and if this cannot be achieved, to at least mitigate the slaughter and destruction. In Medieval Europe, the Church managed to impose a certain restraint, sometimes replacing a war by arbitration. Institutions such as chivalry had the advantage of limiting the forms of conflict, and excluding the civilian population from the fighting. This latter aspect was finally shattered by "total" war, instituted in 1939. From that time on, it has become natural to regard the bombardment of cities as an ordinary act of war. Yet even at that awful state, nations still try to limit war, acting to exclude chemical, biological, and nuclear weapons, for instance.

Irregular warfare is unfortunately yet another component of war. Here, too, distinctions can be made. An irregular or paramilitary force can limit its action to attacks on military installations and to attempts against the leadership of the enemy. The various resistance movements acting against German occupation during the Second World War directed their attacks towards German units, communication networks, roads, bridges, etc. There were no attacks on German schools or homes. Compare this with the present policy of the "Provisional Wing of the IRA" in Britain: bombs in the subway meant to hit civilian passers-by. The IRA-failed action against the British Prime Minister in the summer of 1984 is perhaps their first guerrilla action in Britain, after many terrorist acts. The same goes for the actions of the Puerto-Rican Independence Fighters, who put bombs in civilian airports.

There are two kinds of irregular fighters, and sometimes the distinction between "guerrillas" and "terrorists" represents these two types. The original guerrillas were Spanish irregulars ambushing Napoleonic units. The term "terror" has a connotation of unmitigated slaughter. Unfortunately, the two terms are now exploited in a distorted fashion. The BBC terms the IRA irregulars "terrorists," but the same actions when perpetrated by the PLO in Israel are termed "guerrilla-operations." The irregular who hits me is a terrorist, but the one who hits people I do not like is a guerrilla.

Making the more honest and precise distinction, I would say that present irregular actions by the PLO or their Shi'ite allies in Lebanon against the Israeli Army are guerrilla actions. They are aimed at soldiers. So were the Shi'ite suicide-squad attacks on the U.S. Marines and French units. On the other hand, the same PLO groups acting as they do on Israeli territory--putting bombs in civilian buses and killing school children--these are terrorists of the worst type. In 17 years of Israeli presence in Judea and Samaria there have been few attempts to hit the Israeli Army, but many hundreds or thousands of actions against civilians.

All three Israeli paramilitary organizations which fought the British in 1946-1948 acted as guerrillas, hitting only the military or the government. The Hagana under Ben Gurion's guidance blew up bridges, and other targets even before it limited its actions to the protection of illegal immigration landings and unauthorized settlement erections, after the arrest of the leadership on the June 29, 1946. The Irgun Zvai Leumi under Raziel and Menachem Begin attacked police stations, military airfields, and other objectives. The Fighters for the Freedom of Israel, headed by Itzhak Shamir, ambushed military units and killed Lord Moyne, the British Cabinet representative in the Middle East responsible for the denial of refuge to illegal immigration ships.

I have made the distinction between guerrilla and terrorist acts upon the arrest of the Jewish settlers' vigilance group in the spring of 1984. Their first action in 1980 against the members of the PLO-connected "Palestinian Arab Committee for National Guidance" was highly selective, hitting precisely the leaders who incited the anti-Jewish rioting and killing. However, the 1983 attack on the Islamic Religious University in Hebron (killing three Arab students in retaliation for the killing of eight Jewish students of the Jewish Religious College) was blind revenge. As to the mining of Arab buses in Jerusalem, as a retaliation for the bomb that killed two Jewish schoolgirls in a Jerusalem bus earlier in the year--had the bombs not been dismantled, they might have resulted in the deaths of many innocents. It is interesting to note that when I made the distinction citing the PLO in Lebanon as a case where the targets (Israeli soldiers) were more justifiable in terms of the rules of irregular war, the Israeli New Left did not criticize my definition. When, however, I made the same distinction in classifying the actions of the Jewish vigilantes, I was unamimously accused of encouraging terrorism.

To summarize, even irregular warfare can be kept somewhat cleaner, avoiding the slaughter of innocents.

CONCLUSION

Terrorists and Freedom Fighters

Trying to emphasize the difference of terrorists versus freedom fighters, the following characteristics must be considered in analysing the meaning, consequences and remedies to these contemporary phenomena:

1. Freedom fighters are engaged in selective forms of violence directed against colonial or dictatorial regimes when all political and legal steps, both on the domestic and international levels, have been exhausted.

2. Such selective violence is directed against administrative and military buildings and agents of the power they claim to fight. It never includes civilians as targets and is used to the minimum extent possible--and this distinguishes the methods used by freedom fighters from the indiscriminate violence used by terrorists.

3. As against this, terrorism is the threat and use of undiscernable and unrestrained psychological and physical extra-legal force--including intimidation, coercion, repression, and, ultimately, destruction of human lives and property--for the purpose of attaining political goals.

4. Terrorist actions are intended to destroy, shock, stun and intimidate a target group wider than the immediate victims.

5. Terrorists act in complete disregard of fundamental human rights and a typical feature is an organized attack on innocent victims, frequently bystanders who have no direct connection to a particular cause or conflict.

6. Contemporary terrorism constitutes criminal behavior. While holding contempt for the legal and moral norms of democratic societies these outlaws glorify violent deeds for the sake of "higher" principles and goals.

7. Terrorist attacks are contrary to international law and flout the letter and spirit of the UN Charter. No claim to act on behalf of attaining freedom can justify terrorism as defined herein.

This document was prepared by a committee of the participants in the Inter-University Conference on Underground Movements: 'Terrorists or Freedom Fighters?" held at Hebrew University, Jerusalem, Israel (31st January–2nd February 1984), under the auspices of

-- Bar Ilan University, Ramat Gan, Israel;
-- State University of New York, NY, USA;
-- University of Chicago, IL, USA;
-- Tel Aviv University, Tel Aviv, Israel;
-- The Department of Education and Culture in the Diaspora, W.Z.O., Jerusalem.

BIBLIOGRAPHY

Adeniran, Tunde and Alexander, Yonah, eds. *International Violence*. New York: Praeger Publishers, 1983.

Alexander, Yonah, ed. *International Terrorism: National, Regional, and Global Perspectives*. New York: Praeger Publishers, 1976.

_____. *The Role of Communications in the Middle East Conflict: Ideological and Religious Aspects*. New York: Praeger Publishers, 1973.

_____; Browne, Marjorie; Nanes, Ann and Allen, eds. *Control of Terrorism*. Crane Russak and Company, 1979.

_____; Carlton, David; Wilkinson, Paul, eds. *Terrorism: Theory and Practice*. Boulder: Westview Press, 1979.

_____ and Ebinger, Charles K., eds. *Political Terrorism and Energy: The Threat and Response*. New York: Praeger Publishers, 1982.

_____ and Friedlander, Robert A., eds. *Self-Determination: National, Regional, and Global Perspective*. Boulder: Westview Press, 1979.

_____ and Gleason, John M., eds. *Behavioral and Quantitative Perspectives on Terrorism*. Elmsford, NY: Pergamon Press, 1981.

_____ and Kilmarx, Robert A., eds. *Political Terrorism and Business: The Threat and Response.* New York: Praeger Publishers, 1982.

_____ and Kittrie, Nicholas. *Crescent and Star: Arab-Israeli Perspectives on the Middle East Conflict.* New York: Ams Press, 1972.

_____ and Myers, Kenneth A., eds. *Terrorism in Europe.* New York: St. Martin's Press, 1982.

_____ and O'Day, Alan., eds. *Terrorism in Ireland.* New York: St. Martin's Press, 1984.

_____ and Seymour, M. Finger, eds. *Terrorism: Interdisciplinary Perspectives.* Maidenhead: McGraw Hill Book Co., 1978.

Asmal, Kader. "The Legal Status of National Liberation Movements (with particular reference to South Africa)," *United Nations Centre Against Apartheid, Seminar,* Lagos, Nigeria, 13-16 August 1984. Doc. No. 84-17233.

Bassiouni, M. Cherif, ed. *International Terrorism and Political Crimes.* Springfield, IL: Thomas, 1975.

Baumann, Carol Edler. *The Diplomatic Kidnappings.* The Hague: Nijhoff, 1973.

Becker, Jillian. *Hitler's Children.* London and New York: Panther, 1978.

Begin, Menachem. *The Revolt.* Tel Aviv: Steimatzky, 1983.

Bell, J. Bowyer. *The Myth of the Guerrilla: Revolutionary Theory and Malpractice.* New York: Knopf, 1971.

_____. *On Revolt*. Cambridge: Harvard University Press, 1976.

_____. *The Secret Army: The IR A, 1916-1974*. Cambridge: MIT Press, 1974.

_____. *Terror Out of Zion: The Irgun, Lehi, Stern and the Palestine Underground, 1929-1949*. New York: St. Martin's Press, 1977.

_____. *Transnational Terror*. Washington, DC: American Enterprise Institute for Public Policy Research, 1975.

Beres, Louis Rene. *Terrorism and Global Security: The Nuclear Threat*. Boulder: Westview Press, 1979.

Buckley, D. Alan and Olson, Daniel D., eds. (special consulting editor, Stephen Sloan). *International Terrorism: Current Research and Future Directions*. Wyne, NJ: Avery Publishing Group, 1980.

Burton, Anthony M. *Urban Terrorism: Theory, Practice and Response*. New York: The Free Press, 1975.

Carlton, David and Schaerf, Carlo, eds. *Contemporary Terror: Studies in Sub-state Violence*. London: Macmillan, 1981.

_____ and _____, eds. *International Terrorism and World Security*. London: Croom Helm, 1975.

Chailand, Gerald. *The Palestinian Resistance*. Baltimore: Penguin, 1972.

Clark, Richard C. *Technological Terrorism*. New York: Devin-Adair, 1978.

Clutterbuck, Richard L. *Guerrillas and Terrorists*. London: Faber and Faber, 1977.

_____. *Kidnap and Ransom: The Response*. London and Boston: Faber and Faber, 1978.

_____. *Living with Terrorism*. New York: Arlington House Publishers, 1975.

Crelinsten, Ronald S.; Laberge-Altemeja, Danielle; Szabo, Denis, eds. *Terrorism and Criminal Justice*. Lexington, MA: Lexington Books, 1978.

Crenshaw, Martha, ed. *Terrorism, Legitimacy, and Power: The Consequences of Political Violence*. Wesleyan University Press, 1983.

Crozier, Brian. *The Study of Conflict*. London: The Institute for the Study of Conflict, 1974.

Debray, R. *Revolution in the Revolution*. New York: Monthly Review Press, 1967.

_____. *Strategy for Revolution*. Harmondsworth: Penguin, 1973.

Demaris, Ovid. *Brothers in Blood: The International Network*. New York: Scribner, 1977.

Dobson, Christopher. *Black September: Its Short, Violent History*. New York: MacMillan, 1974.

_____ and Payne, Ronald. *Counterattack: The West's Battle Against the Terrorists*. New York: Facts on File, 1982.

_____ and _____. *The Terrorists: Their Weapons, Leaders and Tactics*. New York: Facts on File, 1979.

_____ and _____. *The Weapons of Terror: International Terrorism at Work*. London and Basingstoke. MacMillan, 1979.

Elliot, John D. and Gibson, Leslie K., eds. *Contemporary Terrorism: Selected Readings*. Gaithersburg: International Association of Chiefs of Police, 1978.

Evans, Ernest. *Calling a Truce to Terror: The American Response to International Terrorism*. Westport, CN: Greenwood Press, 1979.

Francis, Samuel T. *The Soviet Strategy of Terror*. Washington, DC: Heritage Foundation, 1981.

Freedman, Lawrence Zelic and Alexander, Yonah. *Perspectives on Terrorism*. Wilmington, DE: Scholarly Resources, 1983.

Friedlander, Robert A. *Terrorism: Documents of International and Local Control*. Dobbs Ferry, NY: Oceana Publications, 1979, v. 2.

Guevara, Ernesto. *Che Guevara on Guerrilla Warfare*. Translated by Harries-Clichy Peterson. New York: Praeger, 1961.

_____. *Guerrilla Warfare*. New York: Random House, 1961.

Guillen, Abraham. *Philosophy of the Urban Guerrilla*. Translated by D.C. Hodge. New York: Morrow, 1973.

Gurr, Ted Robert. *Cross-National Studies of Civil Violence*. Washington, DC; American University Center of Research in Social Systems, 1969.

_____. *Why Men Rebel*. Princeton: University Press, 1970.

Hacker, Frederick J. *Crusaders, Criminals, Crazies: Terror and Terrorism in Our Time*. New York: Norton, 1976.

Hinze, Paul B. *The Plot to Kill the Pope*. New York: Scribner's, 1983.

Hutchinson, Martha Crenshaw. *Revolutionary Terrorism: The FLN in Algeria, 1954-62*. Stanford, CA: Hoover Institution Press, 1978.

Hyams, Edward. *Terrorist and Terrorism*. New York: St. Martin's Press, 1974.

Katz, Shmuel. *Days of Fire*. New York: Doubleday, 1966.

Kupperman, Robert H. and Trend, D. *Terrorism: Threat, Reality, Response*. Stanford, CA: Hoover Institution Press, 1979.

Laqueur, Walter. *Guerrilla: A Historical and Critical Study*. Boston: Little, Brown, 1976.

_____. *Terrorism*. Boston: Little, Brown, 1977.

_____, ed. *Terrorism Readers: A Historical Anthology*. Philadelphia: Temple University Press, 1978.

Lewis, Bernard. *The Assassins: A Radical Sect in Islam*. New York: St. Martin's Press, 1960.

Liston, Robert A. *Terrorism*. Nashville: Nelson, 1977.

Livingston, Maurius, ed. *International Terrorism in the Contemporary World*. Westport, CT: Greenwood Press, 1978.

Livingstone, Neil C. *The War Against Terrorism*. Lexington, MA: Lexington Books, 1982.

Lodge, Juliet, ed. *Terrorism: A Challenge to the State*. New York: St. Martin's Press, 1981.

Mallin, Jay. *Terror and Urban Guerrillas: A Study of the Tactics and Documents*. Coral Gables, FL: University of Miami Press, 1971.

_____. *Terror in Vietnam*. Princeton: Van Nostrand, 1966.

Mao Tse-tung. *Basic Tactics*. New York: Praeger, 1966.

_____. *On Guerrilla Warfare*. New York: Praeger, 1961.

Marighella, Carlos. *Minimanual of the Urban Guerrilla*. Havana: Tricontinental, n.d.

Mickolus, Edward F., Compiler. *The Literature of Terrorism: A Selected Annotated Bibliography*. Westport, CT: Greenwood Press, 1980.

Miller, Abraham H. *Terrorism and Hostage Negotiations*. Boulder, CO: Westview Press, 1980.

Morris, Michael. *Terrorism*. Cape Town: H. Timmins, 1971.

Moss, Robert. *Urban Guerrillas*. London: Maurice Temple Smith Ltd., 1972.

_____. *The War for the Cities*. New York: Coward, McCann and Geoghegan, 1972.

Netanyahu,   Benjamin,   ed. *International   Terrorism: Challenge and Response*. Jerusalem: Jonathan Institute Press, 1978.

O'Ballance, Edgar. *Terror in Ireland: The IRA and the Heritage of Hate*. San Rafael, CA: Presidio Press, 1981.

Paine, Lauran. *The Terrorists*. London: Hale, 1975.

Parry, Albert. *Terrorism: From Robespierre to Arafat*. New York: Vanguard Press, 1976.

Rapoport, David C.   *Assassination and Terrorism*. Toronto: Canadian Broadcasting Corp., 1971.

_____ and Alexander, Yonah, eds. *The Morality of Terrorism: Religious   and   Secular   Justifications*. Elmsford, NY: Pergamon Press, 1982.

Schamis, Gerardo Jorge. *War and Terrorism in International   Affairs*. New Brunswick, NJ: Transaction Books, 1980.

Shaw, Jennifer, ed. *Ten Years of Terrorism: Collected Views*. London: Royal United Services for Defense Studies. New York: Crane Russak, 1979.

Sloan, Stephen. *Simulating Terrorism*. Norman, OK: University of Oklahoma Press, 1981.

Sobel, Lester A., ed. *Political Terrorism*. New York: Facts on File, 1975.

_____. *Political Terrorism, 1974-1978*, *v. 2*. New York: Facts on File, 1975.

Sterling, Claire. *The Terror Decade: A Biopsy of International Terrorism, 1970-1980*. New York: Holt, Rinehart, and Winston, c. 1981.

_____. *The Terror Network*. New York: Holt, Rinehart, and Winston, 1981.

Stohl, Michael, ed. *The Politics of Terrorism*. New York: M. Dekker, c. 1979.

Tavin, Eli and Alexander, Yonah, eds. *Psychological Warfare and Propaganda: Irgun Documentation*. Wilmington, DE: Scholarly Resources, 1982.

Turi, Robert T., *et al.* *Descriptive Study of Aircraft Hijacking*. Huntsville, Texas: Institute of Contemporary Corrections and the Behavioral Sciences, 1972.

United Nations, General Assembly, Ad Hoc Committee on International Terrorism. *Report*. New York: United Nations, 1973.

Van den Haag, Ernest. *Political Violence and Civil Disobedience*. New York: Harper and Row, 1972.

Walter, Eugene Victor. *Terror and Resistance: A Study of Political Violence*. London and New York: Oxford University Press, 1972.

Wardlaw, Grant. *Political Terrorism: Theory, Tactics, and Counter Measures*. New York: Cambridge University Press, 1983.

Watson, Francis M. *Political Terrorism: The Threat and the Response*. Washington, DC: R.B. Luce, 1976.

Wilkinson, Paul. *Political Terrorism*. New York: Wiley, 1975.

_____. *Terrorism and the ·Liberal State*. New York: Wiley, 1979.

_____. *Terrorism Versus Liberal Democracy: The Problem of Response*. London: Institute for the Study of Conflict, 1976.

Wolf, John B. *Fear of Fear: A Survey of Terrorist Operations and Controls in Societies*. New York: Plenum Press, 1981.

U.S. CONGRESS

U.S. Congress, House, Committee on Foreign Affairs, Subcommittee on the Near East and South Asia. *International Terrorism*. Washington, DC: GPO, 1974.

U.S. Congress, House, Committee on Internal Security. *Terrorism*. Washington, DC: GPO, 1974.

U.S. Congress, House, Committee on International Relations. *International Terrorism*. Washington, DC: GPO, 1978.

U.S. Congress, House, Committee on Public Works and
Transportation, Subcommittee on Aviation, Aircraft
Piracy. *International Terrorism*. Washington, DC:
GPO, 1979.

U.S. Congress, Senate, Committee on Foreign Relations,
Subcommittee on Foreign Assistance. *International
Terrorism*. Washington, DC: GPO, 1977.

U.S. Congress, Senate, Committee on Government Affairs.
An Act to Combat International Terrorism. Washington, DC: GPO, 1978.

U.S. Congress, Senate, Committee on Government Affairs.
Omnibus Antiterrorism Act of 1979. Washington, DC:
GPO, 1979.

U.S. Congress, Senate, Committee on the Judiciary,
Subcommittee on Criminal Laws and Procedures. *The
Terrorist and His Victim, July 21, 1977*. Washington,
DC: GPO, 1977.

U.S. Congress, Senate, Committee on the Judiciary,
Subcommittee on Criminal Laws and Procedures. *West
Germany's Political Response to Terrorism*. Washing-
ton, DC: GPO, 1978.

U.S. Congress, Senate, Committee on the Judiciary,
Subcommittee to Investigate the Administration of the
Internal Security Act and Other Internal Security
Laws. *Terroristic Activity*. Washington, DC: GPO,
1974.

U.S. Congress, Senate, Committee on the Judiciary,
Subcommittee to Investigate the Administration of the

Internal Security Act and Other Internal Security
Laws. *Trotskyite Terrorist International*. Washington, DC: GPO, 1975.

U.S.   Congress,   Senate,   Committee   on   the   Judiciary,
Subcommittee on Security and Terrorism.   *The Role of
Cuba in International Terrorism and Subversion*.   97th
Cong., 2d sess, Washington, DC: GPO, 1982.

U.S.   Congress,   Senate,   Committee   on   the   Judiciary,
Subcommittee on Security and Terrorism.   *Soviet, East
German and Cuban Involvement in Fomenting Terrorism
in Southern Africa*.   97th Cong., 2d sess., Washington,
DC: GPO, 1982.

U.S.   Congress,   Senate,   Committee   on   the   Judiciary,
Subcommittee on Security and Terrorism.   *The Role of
the Soviet Union, Cuba, and East Germany in Fomenting
Terrorism in Southern Africa, Addendum*.   v. 2., 97th
Cong., 2d sess., Washington, DC: GPO, 1982.

U.S.   Congress,   Senate,   Committee   on   the   Judiciary,
Subcommittee on Security and Terrorism.   *Terrorism:
Origins, Direction, and Support*.   Washington, DC:
GPO, 1981.

U.S.   Congress,   Senate,   Committee   on   the   Judiciary,
Subcommittee on Security and Terrorism.   *Terrorism:
The Turkish Experience*. 97th Cong., 1st sess.,
Washington, DC: GPO, 1981.

U.S. MILITARY SOURCES

Commanders Guide to Terrorism Counteraction, Brigade and Battalion Commanders. Pre-command Course, compiled by Jon Michael, Captain, Inf. (84-0340). n.d.

National Security Affairs Institute, National Defense University. *The 1980s: Decade of Confrontation? The Eighth National Security Affairs Conference, 1981 Proceedings.* Fort Lesley J. McNair, Washington, DC: 1981.

U.S. Air Force, Air Force Academy Library. *Terrorism.* Colorado Springs: U.S. Air Force Academy Library, 1977.

U.S. Air Force, Air University, Maxwell Air Force Base, Air Command and Staff College. *Unconventional Warfare: The Hidden Challenge.* n.d.

U.S. Department of the Army, Command and General Staff College, Department of Joint and Combined Operations. *Readings on Terrorism.* October 1980, (82-0471).

U.S. Department of the Army, Command and General Staff College. Terrorism Counteraction Office, Department of Joint and Combined Operations. *Readings on Terrorism.* Compiled by Jon Michael, Captain, Inf., October 1983 (84-0239).

U.S. Department of the Army, Headquarters, Criminal Investigation Command. *Personal Security Assessments.* January 30, 1983 (CID Pamphlet).

U.S. Department of the Army, Headquarters. *Personnel Security Precautions Against Acts of Terrorism.* (PAM 190-52, June 1978).

U.S. Department of the Army, INSCOM, Counterintelligence/Signal Security Battalion, Fort Sam Houston, Texas. *Tips for Countering Terrorism*. 902d Military Intelligence Group, 6 March 1981.

U.S. Department of the Army, Military Police School. *Countering Terrorism on U.S. Army Installations*. Fort McClellan, Alabama, n.d.

U.S. Department of the Army, Military Police Headquarters, Forces Command, Fort McPherson, Georgia. *Countering Terrorism and Other Major Disruptions on Military Installations* (Supplement 1 to AR 190-52), (effective 15 August 1983).

U.S. Department of the Army, Military Police School. *Use of Barriers (To Deny High Speed Approach) In Countering Terrorism Situations*. Field Circular 19-112.

U.S. Department of Defense, Department of the Army, Headquarters. *Personnel Security Precautions Against Acts of Terrorism*. June 1978.

U.S. Department of Defense. *Protection of DOD Personnel Against Terrorism Acts*. April, 1983 (DOD 2000.12-H)

MISCELLANEOUS UNITED STATES GOVERNMENT DOCUMENTS

Law Enforcement Assistance Administration. *Facing Tomorrow's Terrorist Incident Today*. Report prepared by Robert Kupperman, Washington, DC: October 1977.

National Advisory Committee on Criminal Justice Standards and Goals, Task Force on Disorders and Terrorism. *Report.* Washington, DC: GPO, 1976.

National Commission on the Causes and Prevention of Violence. *Assassination and Political Violence.* J.F. Kirkham and S. Levy, Washington, DC: GPO, 1969.

National Governor's Association, Emergency Preparedness Project, Center of Policy Research. *Domestic Terrorism.* Washington, DC: GPO, 1979.

U.S. Central Intelligence Agency, Directorate of Intelligence. *International Terrorism in 1976.* Washington, DC: CIA, 1977, 1978.

U.S. Central Intelligence Agency, National Foreign Assessment Center. *International Terrorism in 1978.* Washington, DC: CIA, 1979.

U.S. Department of Commerce, National Technical Information Service, Foreign Broadcast Information Service. *Daily Reports.*

U.S. Department of Justice, FBI, Terrorist Research and Analytical Center, Terrorism Section, Criminal Investigative Division. *FBI Analysis of Terrorist Incidents in the United States.* 1983.

U.S. Department of Justice, Law Enforcement Assistance Administration. *Prevention of Terroristic Crimes: Security Guidelines for Business, Industry, and Other Organizations.* Prepared by Arthur J. Bilek, Washington, DC: GPO, May 1976.

U.S. Department of State, Bureau of Public Affairs. *Combatting Terrorism*. Washington, DC: September 1982.

U.S. National Security Council, Special Coordination Committee. *The U.S. Government Antiterrorism Program, An Unclassified Summary Report*. Prepared by the Executive Committee on Terrorism, June 1979.

ARTICLES IN JOURNALS

Alexander, Yonah. Communications Aspects of International Terrorism. *International Problems*, v. 16, n. 1-2, Spring 1977, pp 55-60.

_____. The Nature of the PLO: Some International Implications. *Middle East Review*, v. XII, n. 3, Spring 1980, pp 42-51.

_____. Some Perspectives on Terrorism and the Soviet Union. *International Security Review*, v. VII, n. 1, Spring 1982, pp 35-45.

_____. Some Soviet-PLO Linkages. *Middle East Review*, v. XIV, n. 3-4, Spring-Summer 1982, pp 64-69.

_____ and Levine, Herbert M. Prepare for the Next Entebbe. *Chitty's Law Journal*, v. 25, September 1977, pp 240-242.

Beres, Louis Rene. International Terrorism and World Order: The Nuclear Threat. *The Stanford Journal of International Studies*, v. XII, Spring 1977, pp 131-146.

Clutterbuck, Richard. Terrorist International. *Army Quarterly and Defense Journal*, v. 104, January 1974, pp 154–159.

Deakin, T.J. Legacy of Carlos Marighella. *FBI Law Enforcement Bulletin*, v. 43, n. 10, October 1974, pp 19–25.

Dugard, John. Towards the Definition of International Terrorism. *American Journal of International Law*, v. 67, November 1974, pp 94–102.

Elliott, John D. Contemporary Terrorism and the Police Response. *Police Chief*, February 1978, pp 40–43.

Evans, Alona E. Terrorism and Political Crimes in International Law. *The American Journal of International Law*, v. 67, n. 5, November 1973, pp 82–95.

Fearey, Robert A. International Terrorism. *Department of State Bulletin*, v. 74, March 29, 1976, pp 394–403.

Friedlander, Robert A. Terrorism and National Liberation Movements: Can Rights Derive from Wrongs? *Case Western Reserve Journal of International Law*, v. 13, n. 2, Spring 1981, pp 303–308.

Krieger, David M. Terrorists and Nuclear Technology: The Danger is Great, the Question Is Not Whether the Worse Will Happen But Where and How. *Bulletin of the Atomic Scientists*, June 1975, pp 28–34.

Hoffacker, Lewis. The U.S. Government Response to Terrorism: A Global Approach. *Department of State Bulletin*, v. 70, March 18, 1974, pp 274–278.

Hutchinson, Martha Crenshaw. Transnational Terrorism and World Politics. *Jerusalem Journal of International Relations*, v. 1, Winter 1975, pp 109-129.

Jenkins, Brian. International Terrorism: A Balance Sheet. *Survival*, v. 17, July-August 1975, pp 158-164.

Joyner, Christopher. Offshore Maritime Terrorism: International Implications and the Legal Response. *Naval War College Review*, v. XXXVI, n. 4, July-August 1983, pp 14-21.

Laqueur, Walter. Interpretations of Terrorism: Fact, Fiction and Political Science. *Journal of Contemporary History*, v. 12, January 1977, pp 1-42.

Moore, John Norton. Toward Legal Restraints on International Terrorism. *American Journal of International Law*, v. 67, November 1974, pp 88-94.

Romaniecki, Leon. The Soviet Union and International Terrorism. *Soviet Studies*, v. 26, n. 3, July 1974, pp 417-440.

Tanham, George K.; Jenkins, Brian; Weinstein, Eleanor S.; and Sullivan, Gerald. United States Preparation for Future Low-Level Conflict. *Conflict: An International Journal*, v. 1, 1978, pp 1-19.